Graphics
Alive 2

viction:ary

Graphics 2 Alive

First published and distributed by
viction:workshop ltd.

viction:ary™

Unit C, 7th Floor, Seabright Plaza,
9-23 Shell Street, North Point, Hong Kong
Url: www.victionary.com   Email: we@victionary.com

Edited and produced by viction:workshop ltd.

Book design by viction:workshop ltd.
Concepts & art direction by Victor Cheung

Susa (script typeface) sponsored by Hubert Jocham
Slipcase illustrations & opening graphic elements
by Dopludó Collective

ISBN 978-988-17327-0-5

Printed and bound in China

Contents

What?

Foreword

by Francesco Rugi at carnovsky

When I was asked to write a foreword for Graphics Alive 2, I accepted the invitation right away – but almost immediately I realised that the task was much harder than I thought. I always find it quite difficult to talk in general terms about a subject rather than about a specific case!

Apparently there are dozens of good books about the history of graphic design which surely carry more interesting and authoritative points of view than mine – but what really fascinates me about graphic is exactly the way of it being elusive, with its beauty lays on its ambiguity – an ambiguity that may also be embedded in its Greek root that comes from the word graphē, which means 'to write' and also 'to draw'. While I found familiar ideas in Wikipedia in Italian, which approaches the subject by distinguishing 'graphics' from other art forms such as painting or drawing by its nature being 'original' or being 'reproduced', the English Wikipedia on the contrary interprets it as a much huger container, encompassing everything from ancient cave art to Chinese manuscripts, advertising graphics, multinationals' logos and even Frank Gehry's Guggenheim museum at Bilbao as an

Francesco Rugi and Silvia Quintanilla together form carnovsky, a design studio based in Milan.

example of contemporary influence in graphic design. (If we have learned something from *Las Vegas*, the Guggenheim will clearly be one of the greatest examples of 'Duck', i.e. the complete opposite of "decorated sheds" or more precisely 'buildings', where architecture and graphic and, in general, all the plastic arts, live together.) But actually most contemporary buildings seem to be a mere support in lieu of a component for a graphic texture.

So what really makes it difficult to draw a clear line about graphics is the fact that the nature of graphics – its concept and notion per se – is somehow elusive and ambiguous. What is exactly indicated by the term? When does the concept of 'graphic design' come to life? What contributes to the boundaries of this discipline? How does it distinguish itself from, e.g. product design or architecture? Obviously the answer cannot be merely about the predominance of the tridimensional elements over the plain flat ones, but what I want to say is basically everything *is* graphics. And if everything is graphics, it would mean that nothing is graphics and it loses the specific meanings about graphics. That's how I find myself back at the starting point for the discovery of meanings about graphics... with my head quite confused.

For the artist, creating the new may mean choosing the old or the existing.

– R. Venturi, D. Scott Brown, S. Izenour, *Learning from Las Vegas*

Viva la grafica!

To see it is to understand it.

Living in today's society with its explosive visual culture we tend to take graphics for granted. Graphics have become such an obvious part of everyday life, we very rarely stop and consider their true importance. The haze of abundance seems to cloud our visual perspective.

In essence graphics are language. Rather than being merely a convenient addition to our day-to-day communication, graphics form an autonomous ever-expanding linguistic process. They seem to exceed the limits of conventional language in the sense that graphics aren't subjugated to the boundaries of a finite vocabulary. Although cultural properties can be a defining factor, the visible language has the potential to be universal.

Graphics speak to us by tapping into our personal and collective visual libraries where every image conveys a specific range of emotions. Images rely on the eyes for the extraction of meaning

See?

by Pointdextr and Toykyo

instead of our ears. The speed of light far exceeds the slow sound wave therefore information can be transmitted instantly – to see it is to understand it. Graphics do however possess a seemingly ambiguous character as a vessel for meaning. Where the medium assures swift communication, it can also act as a buffer, creating a distance between the observer and the content and thus increasing the chance for objective decision making.

Language has always been a powerful tool for interpreting the world. We try to grasp our surroundings by defining them. One could argue that the very fabric of reality is in fact language. In the case of graphics it seems we try to understand the world by decorating it. The act of creation (actively participating with one's surroundings) is essential in this particular process.

Having experienced the joy of observing, we now find ourselves on the other side of the equation and have become image-makers. If our imagery succeeds in transmitting only one emotion, let it be a smile – a smile that withholds both a whiff of nostalgia that can transport the observer back to their childhood and a glimpse of the future; a vision of a better world.

A revolution of communication has been key in all steps of human evolution. Consciously embracing graphics in all their complexity as a visible language might take us to the next level.

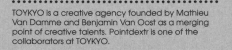

TOYKYO is a creative agency founded by Mathieu Van Damme and Benjamin Van Oost as a merging point of creative talents. Pointdextr is one of the collaborators at TOYKYO.

Title. Vivi Dot Accessories ***Design.*** Vivi Dot ***Photography.***
Kami Shallenberger, Hana Brooks Nation ***Description.***
Handmade accessories featuring bold fabric-covered buttons
transformable into casual statement pieces.

Title. Vivi Dot Accessories **Design.** Vivi Dot
Photography. Kami Shallenberger, Hana Brooks Nation

1. Dotted Oak Tree Ring 2. Tea Cup Ring
3. Tea Time Rings 4. Hamburger Ring on Mustard
5. Giraffe Hair Clips 6. Coquette Necklace
7. Bike Lane Necklace 8. Dotted Mint Bow Necklace

6

7

8

Title. My Own Bag (p.012-015) **Design.**
Bosque studio **Description.** Handprinted
and silkscreened limited edition tote bags.

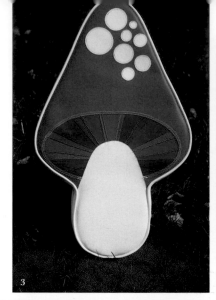

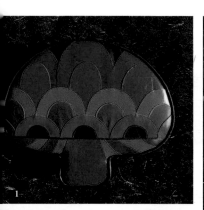

Title. Shroomies & Mushrooms **Design.** Snaggs
Description. Soft-sculptures launched for various
shows, including a duo-show with Arbito and "Make
It or Break It' in Portland, Oregon.

Title. Soggy Bottoms Cereal (on facing page)
Design. Snaggs **Description.** Fake cereal brand
crafted out of felt.

*1. Hazy & Lazy / Rainbow Mushroom   2. Make It or
Break It / Purple Hooded Shroom   3. Make It or Break It /
Yellow Capped Shroom   4. Make It or Break It / Sunny-Side
Shroom   5. Mushroom Fantasy   6. Make It or Break It /
Rainbow Shroom*

"*Looking at my children at breakfast, I'm convinced that if the box was blank, the cereals should be less good!*"

– Kanardo

> "*Most of us need constant stimulation, and that's where graphics come into play. Graphics keep our eyes and brains stimulated!*"
>
> – Snaggs

1

Title. Airbrush Coin Bank
Design. Arbito
Description. Coin banks for Arbito's solo show 'Far Out West' at Super 7.

1. Stink Fry
2. Pink Cosmic Boogie
3. Sad Sap

2

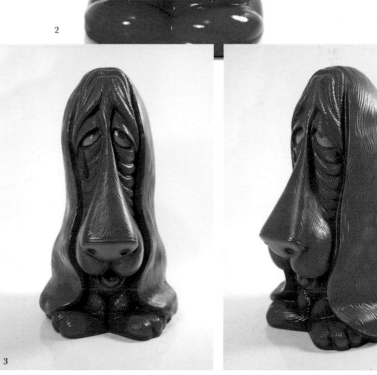

3

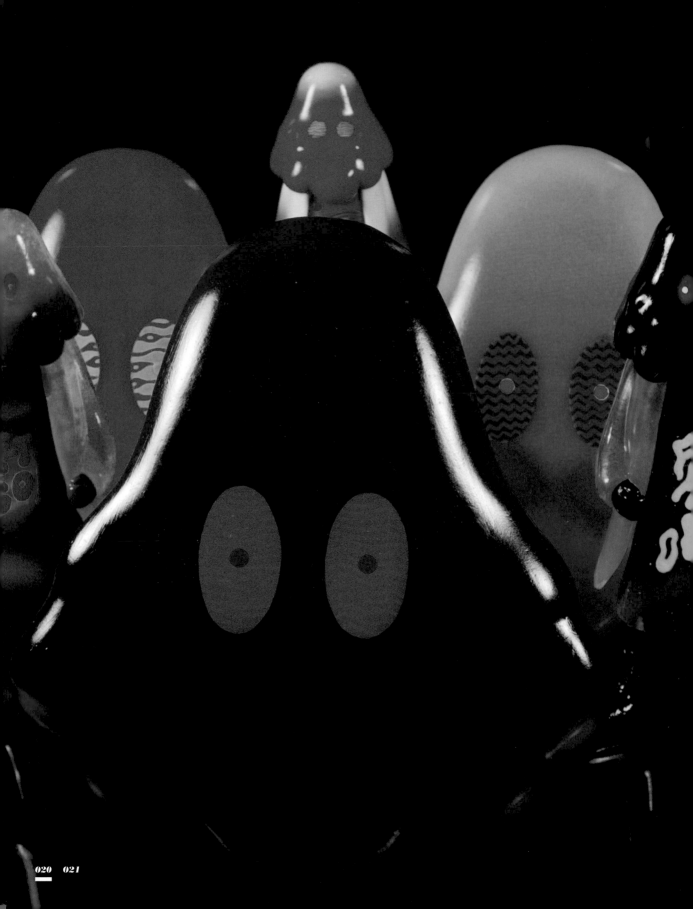

Title. Groovy Glow Seekers   **Design.** Arbito
Description. Resin figure series with embedding
glow in the dark heads inside figures.

Title. Labbitrioshka (above) **Design.** Malotaprojects
Description. Labbit created for collective show "Down
The Bunny Hole" by Rivet Gallery in Columbus, Ohio.

Title. Karu (right) **Design.** Malotaprojects, Elvira H.
Mateu **Description.** Elvira H. Mateu was responsible for
Karu's hair with silver and Malota had sewed him nice.

Title. Momo **Design.** Malotaprojects
Description. Custom toy for private collector.

"Each single element around your eyes talks with you... this world is really the best project from a superstar art director."

– Happy lovers town

Title. Malota Plushes ***Design.*** Malotaprojects
Description. Self-initiated characters designed
and handsewed by Malota.

Title. SUMMER IN NY IS FUCKED *Design.* TOYKYO,
Craig Redman@Rinzen *Description.* Limited edition
plastic resin sculpture coated with glossy laquer paint for
Craig Redman, Rinzen and Darcel.

Title. BILLY THE CONE, BILLY THE CONE JR.
Design. TOYKYO, Bue **Description.** Limited edition
sculptures made by fiberglass and plastic resin.

Title. POPFRUIT *Design*. TOYKYO, Parra
Description. Numbered and signed limited
edition polyester sculptures.

Title. NOT SO HAPPY BIRD (on facing page)
Design. TOYKYO, Parra *Description*.
Twenty-two cm in height. Limited edition
porcelain birds packed in handscreened and
numbered boxes.

Title. KEEP THE FLAME ALIVE (on facing page)
Design. TOYKYO, Pointdextr **Description.**
Limited edition handmade candles.

Title. VADER PROJECT **Design.** TOYKYO,
Pointdextr, Kaiser **Description.** Custom Darth
Vader helmets.

Title. NIKE AF-1   *Design*. TOYKYO,
Bue, Hell'o Monsters   *Description*. Custom
sneaker design for Nike Air Force One's 25th
anniversary exhibition.

"Graphic is a way of thinking minus language. It is like music, transmitting a mood or an idea in a non-verbal way."

– KnittaPlease

Title. THE GLIMMERS BONGO   **Design.** TOYKYO, Pointdextr
Description. Collaboration headphone design launched with Belgian DJ duo, The Glimmers, commissioned by WeSC.

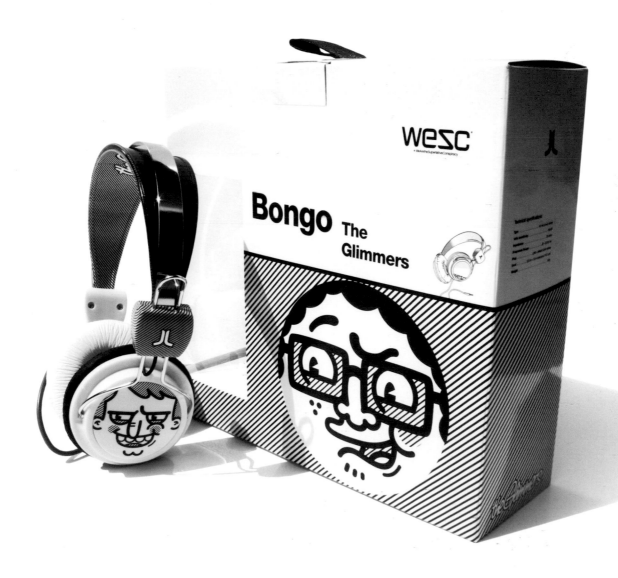

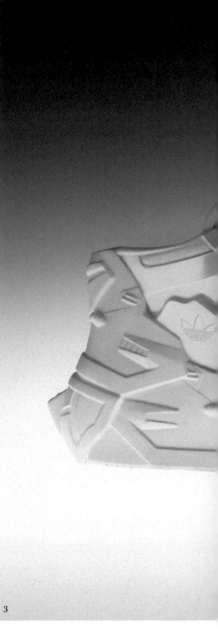

1

2

3

4

5

Title. All Day I Dream About Sneakers   **Design.** Lifelounge
Photography. Chris Tovo   **Retouching.** Todd Riddiford
Description. Sculpted models for a global branding campaign
for adidas Originals, inspired by their brand creeds, 'Impossible Is
Nothing' and 'Celebrate Originality'.

1. Airbag   2. adidas defence   3. adidas robot
4. Tree   5. adidas Midas

Title. P-Rod Boost Mobile   *Design.* David Carvalho
Description. Artwork developed for Boost Mobile for
a special artist edition campaign.

"Graphics are story-tellers – they carry a lot of information, and help us make meaning of our everyday world."

– Mottoform

Title. Russian Dolls Are Bitches   **Design.** TABAS
Description. Typographic designs for a Russian
doll-themed collective exhibition.

Title. Birds In The Sky, Drinkers
Design. TABAS **Description.**
Illustrations for Rossignol snowboards.

Title. Smokers, Birds In The Sky **Design.** TABAS
Description. Illustrations for Rossignol snowboards.

Title. Fear *Design.* Kanardo *Description.*
Artwork series, including a wall painting, a
special tee and a mixed media artwork made for
Ambiguous Clothing.

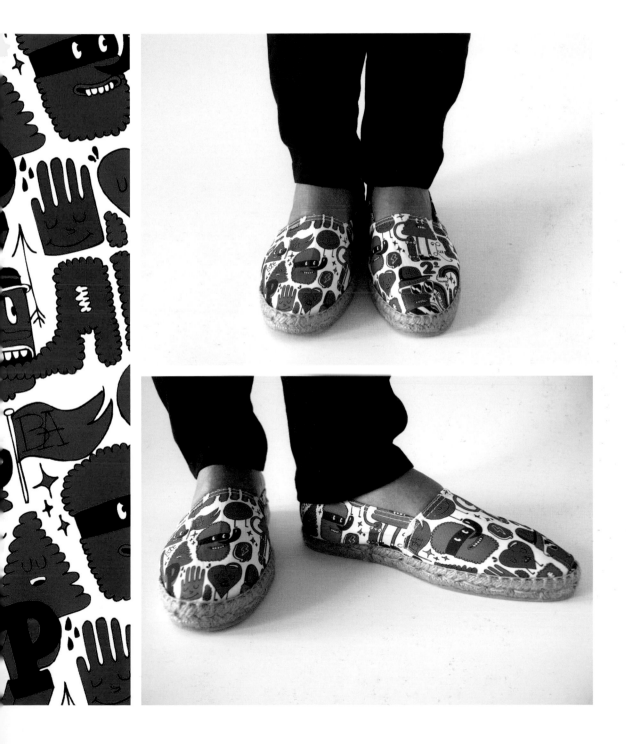

Title. La Peinture C'est Cool (on facing page)   ***Design.*** TABAS,
Type Quatre   ***Description.*** Home decoration composed of a
circle mirror, paint and sticker made in collaboration with interior
decorator, Liza Générale at Type Quatre.

Title. StreetheART   ***Design.*** Staynice   ***Description.***
Handpainted graphic on blanc skateboard for exhibition
"StreetheART" in New York.

"Without graphics we have no identities, no signage… nor interactive design. Graphics help us make sense of the world."

– Ashley Thompson@SHH

Title. Urban Gnome *Design.* Vitamin
Description. Gnomes inspired by London's
street art. Made from bone China.

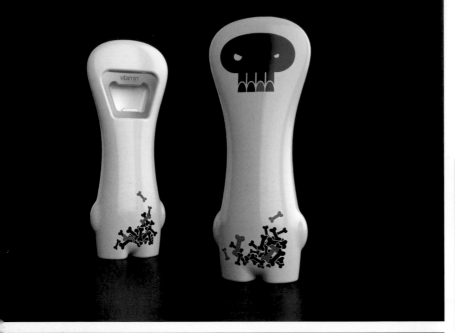

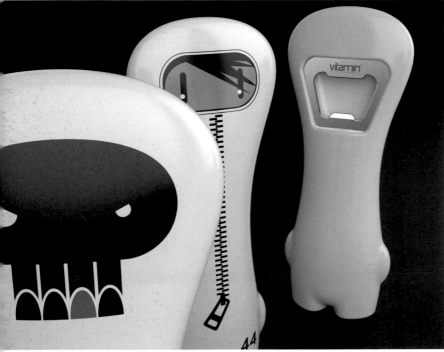

Title. Fang the Freestanding Bottle Opener
Design. Vitamin ***Description.*** Bottle openers as
new members to the Urban Creatures family.

Title. Urban Creature Collection *Design.* Vitamin
Description. Extended family of the Urban Gnomes,
comprised of money box, bottle opener, salt and
pepper shakers and a kitchen timer.

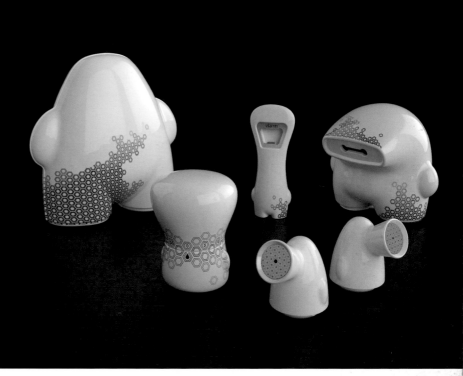

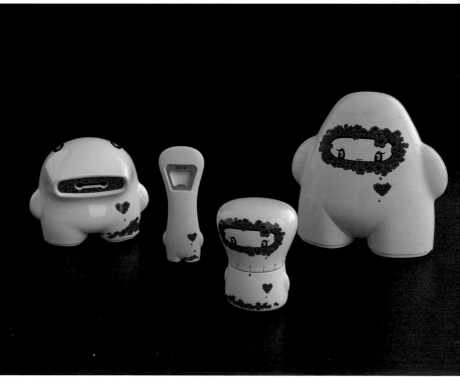

"Graphics connect with us through fashion, branding and advertising. We wouldn't be able to identify most companies without something as basic as a logo."

— Snaggs

Title. Signature Sneakers For Vans   *Design.* Keren Richter
Description. Signature Wellesley Sneakers for Vans Footwear
with two colourways released in fall 08 and spring 09. Project
includes totes, journals and advertising campaign.

VANS®

FEATURING ARTIST COLLABORATION
VANS X KEREN RICHTER

Title. Your Street Dealer ***Design.*** Happy lovers town
Curation. Omar Rashid ***Description.*** Limited artist
tee series for Your Street Dealer.

Title. TOYKYO KIDS **Design.** TOYKYO, Bue, An Oost **Description.** Unisex collection for children aged between two and 12.

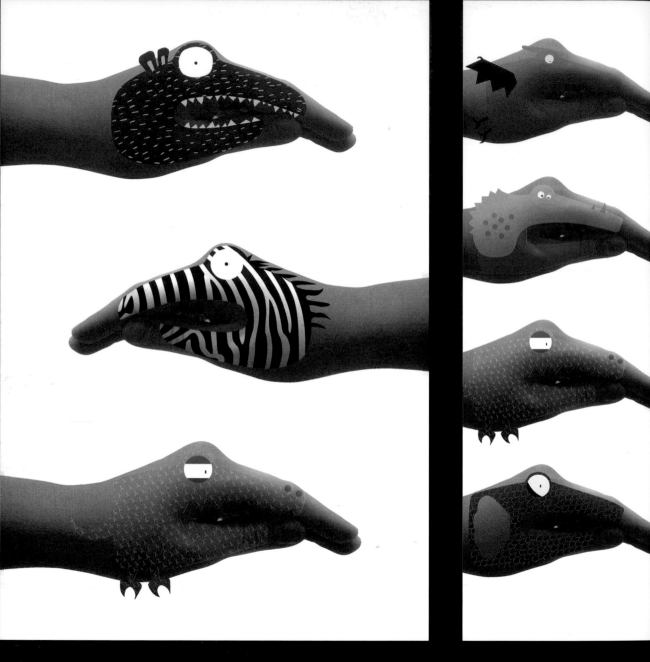

Title. Animal and Monster Hands   *Design.* Héctor Serrano Studio
Description. Removable tattoos able to be transformed on games
and amusing situations. Designed for Worldwide Co.

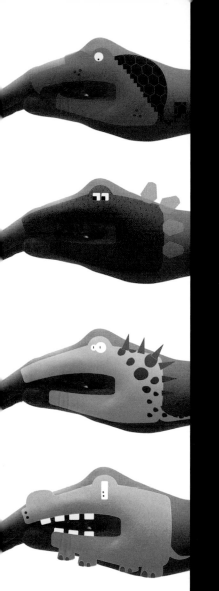

"Graphics is our way of putting our imagination into something that everyone can see... our way of decorating the modern world."

– Bosque Studio

Title. Oilily Bicycle Collection   *Art direction & design.* Studio Kluif – Paul Roeters, Heike Pfisterer
Description. Graphics for Oilily bicycles.

Title. Electra Amsterdam Girard 3i – Madonna (top),
Tree of Life (bottom) ***Design.*** Alexander Girard
Description. Reincarnation of Dutch style city bikes
for Electra Bicycles Company.

Title. The Silence of Love (above) **Art direction.** Eddie Bezalel
Design. Sarah Lynne Graves, No Days Off **Illustration.** Irana
Douer **Description.** Album cover illustrations for Headless Heroes.

Title. EKENDRA / summer collection 09 (left and below)
Art direction & design. Carolina Badaloni **Illustration.**
Irana Douer **Description.** Illustrations and patterns for SOMA.

Title. Handdrawn Ceramic Cup *Design & illustration.*
Irana Douer *Description.* Illustrations on ceramic cups.

Title. Untitled (illustration and pillowcase) *Art direction.*
Third Drawer Down *Design & illustration.* Irana Douer
Description. Illustrations for Third Drawer Down pillowcase.

Title. Display at agete Aoyama   ***Design***. Kiyoshi
Kuroda   ***Description***. Three-dimensional paper-art
for agete's anniversary at the fashion brand's Aoyama
shop. Commissioned by A&S Inc.

"Graphics has an advantage over words. It is their universal nature that transcends borders."

– Malotaprojects

Title. Heather's Pillow Collection   **Design.** Heather Lins Home   **Description.** Modern homes textile designs produced from eco-friendly materials including pure wool felt and faux suede made from recycled bottles.

1. Eye Chart   2. Conversation Pieces   3. Science Project

2

4

1

3

Title. Folky Pillows **Design**. Dopludó Collective
Description. A pillow series to reminisce fairy tales, culture
and folklore of cold Scandinavian countries and Russia.

1. Animalism   2. Mountains   3. Pipe   4. Senior   5. For-rest   6. Folky

6

5

Title. Nesting Doll   *Design.* Dopludó Collective
Description. Themed paintings on Russian nesting
doll. From left to right in the row, the dolls symbolise
kindness, wisdom, a tree-loving spirit, freedom and
distinctiveness.

Title. Qinghuaci Diana f+   ***Design.*** Dorophy Tang
Description. A redesign for vintage Lomography camera,
Diana f+, with Tang's signature Qinghua style, for the
Detrich Collection & Diana Vignettes Exhibition.

Title. Insane ABS ***Design.*** Dorophy Tang
Description. Be@rbrick figure dressed up in the
signature features of traditional Chinese Qinghua
porcelain ware and Tang's Shopping Baby for Charity
Auction for Angel's Smile Foundation.

"Graphics boldly tell of a time when we lived differently... They might even induce nostalgia for an era prior to our materialist, throw-away culture."

– Mottoform

Title. a.m. & p.m Chair Set   ***Design.*** Dorophy Tang
Description. Chairs re-interpreted in Tang's signature
Qinghua style for adidas China.

Title. Drops   ***Design.*** Studio Violet   ***Description.*** Black, matte vinyl wall stickers to deck the walls, mirrors, desks etc.

Title. Circus Violet Porcelain, Katta Poster (on facing page)   ***Design.*** Studio Violet   ***Description.*** Reused porcelain with ceramic decals for a show at Manos in Stockholm, and offset poster.

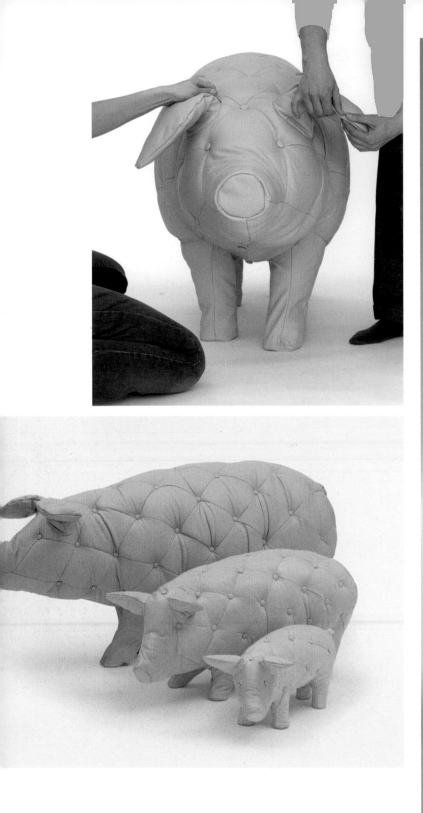

Title. Still Lives **Design.** Fehling & Peiz
Photography. Frederik Busch **Description.**
Life-sized pig family upholstered in leather with
traditional diamond quilting.

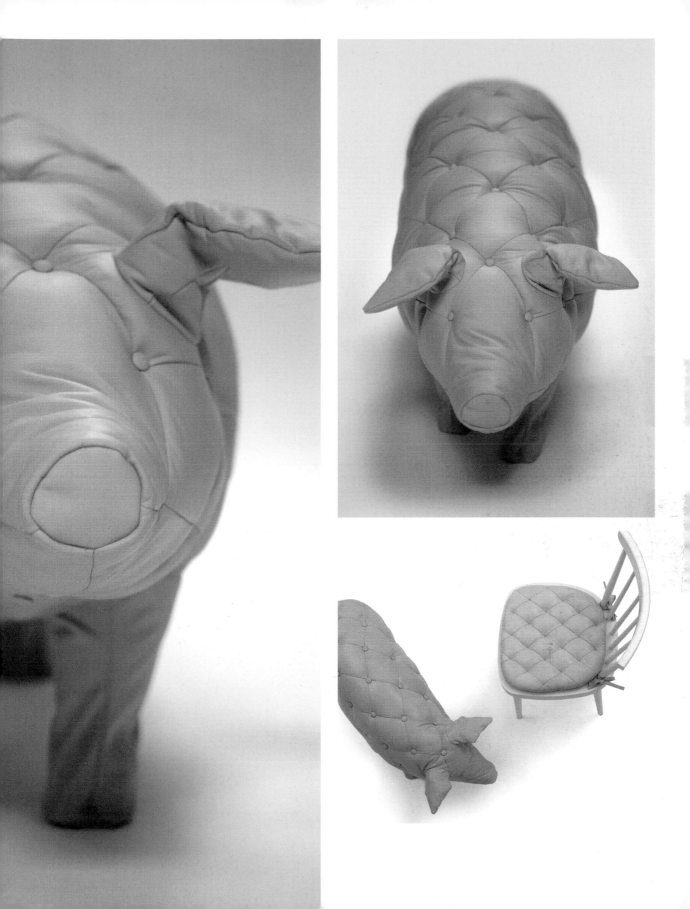

Title. The Rework Collection **Design.** Peter & Sally Nencini
Description. Private commissions to rework chairs with upholstery
and stitching. From left to right are The Point Chair to witness a
little boy's growth; The Tyrella Chair depicting elements of Tyrella
beach in County Down; The Shoe Chair with words from Gaston
Bachelard's "The Poetics of Space"; and the Calligraphic Chairs,
with four dining chairs from the 1960s.

1. The Point Chair   2. The Tyrella Chair   3. The Shoe Chair
4. Calligraphic Chairs

On OPEN weet DOOR. CLOSED DOOR. A Den. THE WILD PULSE that BEYOND in DOOR. OUR CORNER of THE WORLD: O OUR FIRST UNIVERSE

3

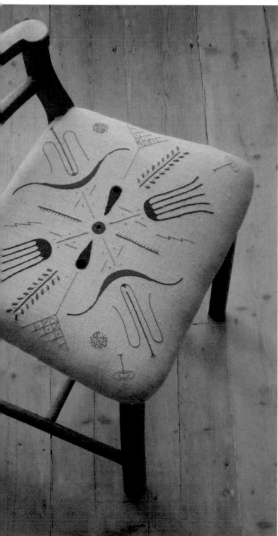

4

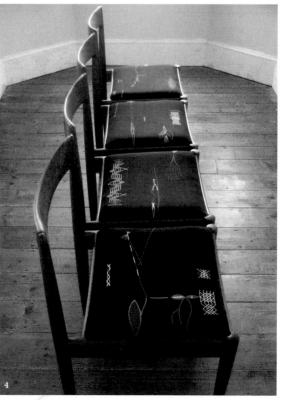

Title. Helsinki Remade ***Design.*** Mottoform
Description. Handprinted vintage linens
inspired by relief patterns found in Art Nouveau
architecture from early 20th century Helsinki.

Title. Porcelain Wall Decor **Design.** Angus &
Celeste **Photography.** Jo Duck **Description.**
Porcelain Wall Tiles slip-cast in special pillow-shaped
moulds; and Wall Birds handcrafted in homage to
the 1950s flying wall ducks.

Title. Winter Scarves ***Design.*** Angus & Celeste
Photography. Jo Duck ***Description.*** Scarves with
porcelain brooch pins and lined with an extra layer
of thick flannelette.

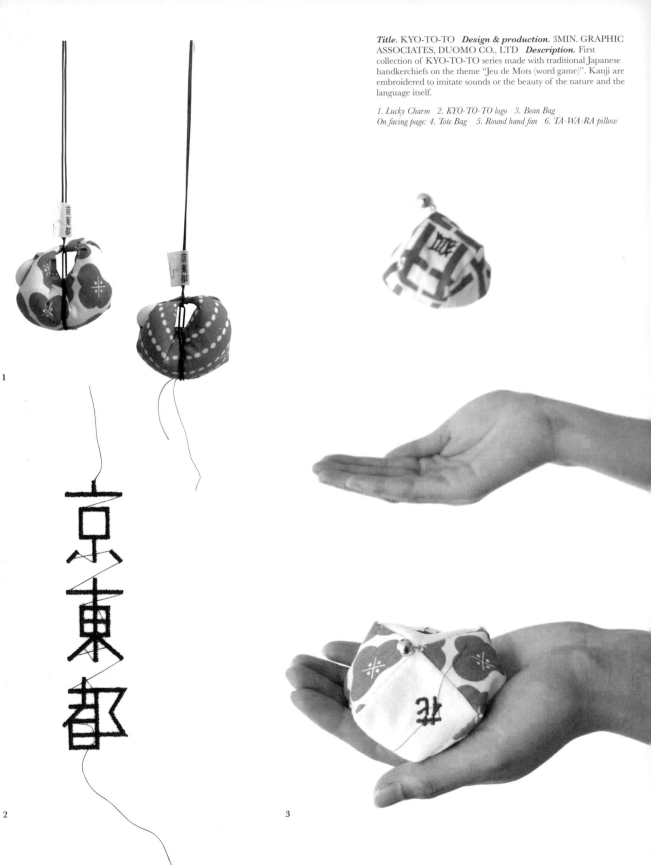

Title. KYO-TO-TO **Design & production.** 3MIN. GRAPHIC ASSOCIATES, DUOMO CO., LTD **Description.** First collection of KYO-TO-TO series made with traditional Japanese handkerchiefs on the theme "Jeu de Mots (word game)". Kanji are embroidered to imitate sounds or the beauty of the nature and the language itself.

1. Lucky Charm   2. KYO-TO-TO logo   3. Bean Bag
On facing page: 4. Tote Bag   5. Round hand fan   6. TA-WA-RA pillow

1

2

3

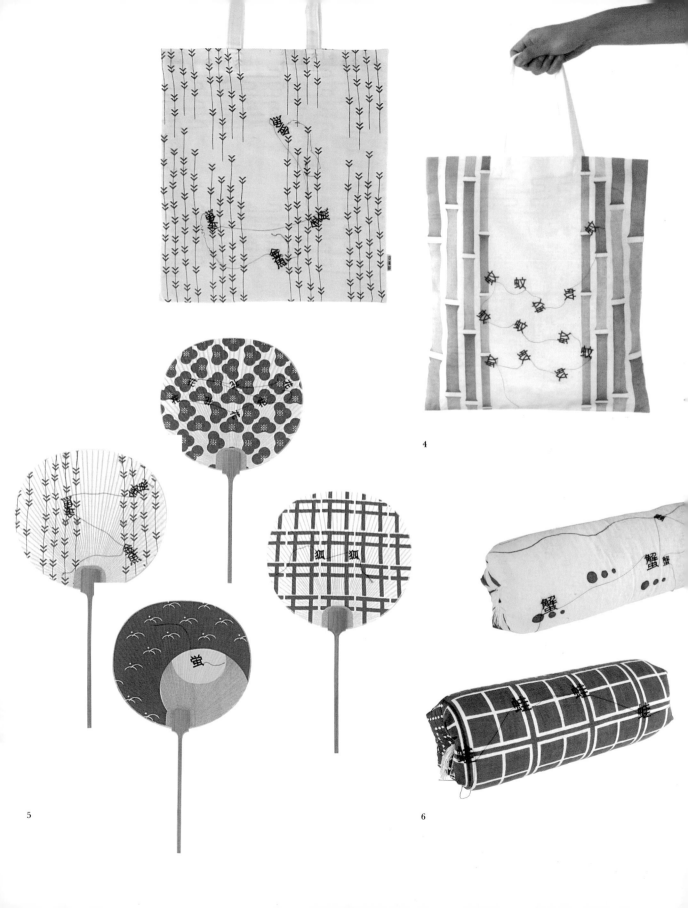

4

5   6

Title. Become A Legend *Design.* Bas van de Poel & Daan van Dam *Description.* Self-initiated premium for 2010 FIFA World Cup. For Dutch supporters to celebrate like the players when the team scores.

Title. Sir Harald **Design.** Studio
Lisa Bengtsson **Description.** Fabric
design as a retrospective of the
designer's great-grandfather's life.

Title. Happy   *Design.* Hanna Melin
Description. Personal work with drawings of
memories from travels and holidays when life
seemed much easier to the artist.

Title. Oss Kvinnor Emellan (Between Us Woman)
Design. Studio Lisa Bengtsson ***Photography.*** Lisa
Björner ***Description.*** Ceramic plates dedicated to
females in a family with a unique story.

"As we perceive the world through our eyes, we visit other artists' 'spaces' and 'worlds'."

– Kristina Sabaite

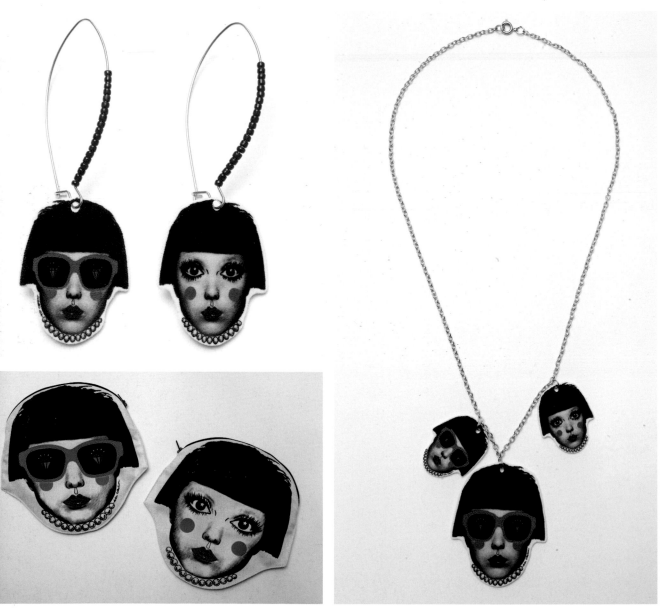

Title. Super Bybie Collection   ***Design.***
Wahahafactory   ***Description.*** Accessories to
take over plastic Barbie's place to cheer up its
owner everyday.

Title. Cosmos   **Design.** Coco Studio
Description. Silk scarves from Coco's
A/W collection 2009/10.

1

3

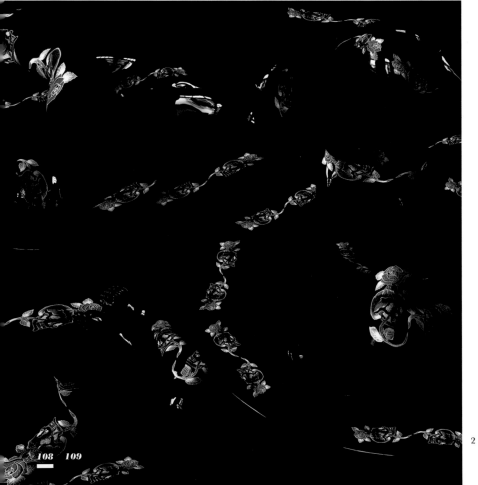

2

Title. Fragile ***Design.*** Kim Joon
Description. Tattoos in digital prints.

1.Fragile-Dragon 2. Fragile-Meiseen
3. Fragile-Skulls . 4.Fragile-Chunhyang on the Limoge

4

1

Title. Fragile **Design.** Kim Joon

*1. Fragile-Herend   2. Fragile-Vileroy & Boch
3. Fragile-Mermaid*

2

3

"Graphics can inspire art and are inspired by art... They are always a part of every human culture."

– Arbito

Title. Manga Ormolu *Design*. Brendan Lee Satish Tang *Description*. Sculpture series created as a fusion of Chinese ceramic traditions, techno-pop graphics and pop culture, such as anime and manga.

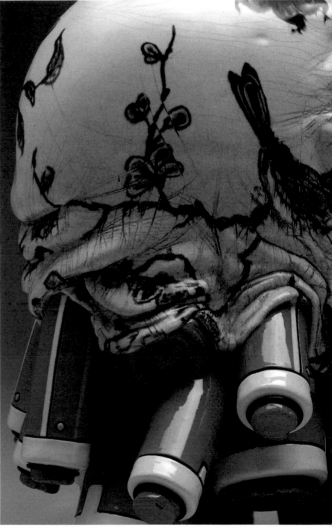

Title. Manga Ormolu ***Design.*** Brendan Lee Satish Tang

Title. COLLARIX *Design.* Tixinda *Photography.*
Miguel Angel Manrique-MANN *Description.*
Handmade jewellery. Winter series inspired by colours
of the Mexican parties and the warmth of textiles.

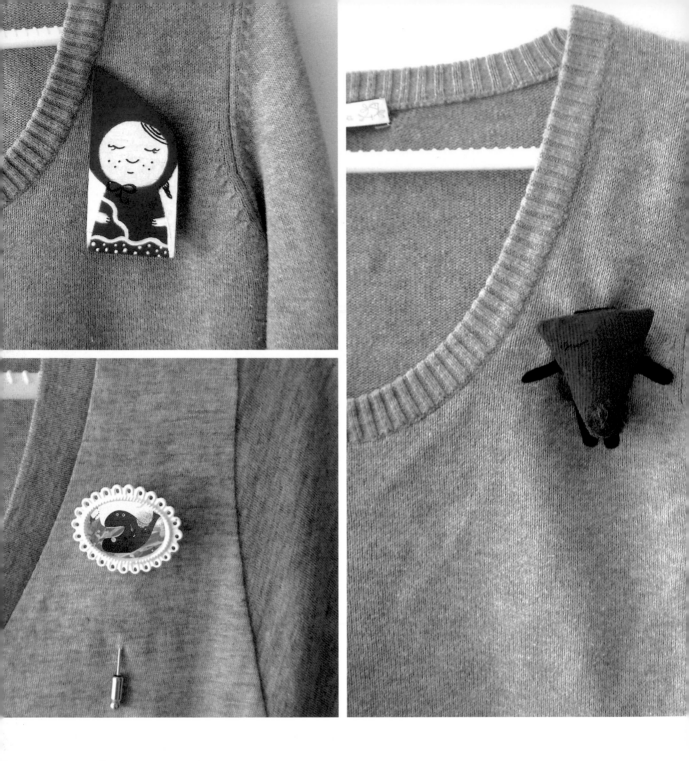

Title. Mini Toys **Design.** Kristina Sabaite
Description. Handmade and handpainted mini
toys as brooches or necklaces, with inspirations
from designer's own illustrations.

Title. One Eye Laughing, The Other Crying. ***Design.*** Anne Marie Skjoldager Jensen ***Photography.*** Brian Buchard, Sacha Maric ***Description.*** Collection using print, colours and shapes to interpret "On the Gallery" by 20th century novelist Franz Kafka. On the Gallery describes the complexity, contradictions and absurdity of the circus world.

Title. One Eye Laughing, The Other Crying.
Design. Anne Marie Skjoldager Jensen
Photography. Brian Buchard, Sacha Maric

Title. One Eye Laughing, The Other Crying.
Design. Anne Marie Skjoldager Jensen
Photography. Brian Buchard, Sacha Maric

Title. DRESS ROCKLOBSTER *Design.* Heal
fashion lab. *Photography.* Cedric Bihr *Description.*
Suit dress in flesh-coloured jersey and lobster embossed
in scarlet silk for A/W collection 2009.

Title. {My Dear} *Design.* Frédérique Morrel
Photography. Philippe Cluzeau *Description.*
Costumes sewed from vintage tapestry collected
by designer for self portraits.

Title. The Sealpelt **Design.** Vík Prjónsdóttir
Photography. Gulli Már **Description.** Wool
blankets for Vikwool inspired by a local folk
story from the neighbourhood of Vikwool, the
knitting factory.

Title. The Snow Blanket (above) **Design.** Vík Prjónsdóttir **Photography.** Gulli Már **Description.** Wool blanket for Víkurprjón. Intended to give isolation and protection to its users like the snow from nature.

Title. The Seal Pelt Remixed by Henrik Vibskov (right) **Design.** Vík Prjónsdóttir, Henrik Vibskov **Photography.** Gulli Már **Description.** Wool blanket re-interpreted by Henrik Vibskov for Víkurprjón and his winter collection.

Title. Shield of Wings, Hidden World, Black or White (left to right) *Design.* Vík Prjónsdóttir *Photography.* Gulli Már *Description.* Wool blankets for Víkurprjón inspired by the grace of sea eagles, a world that most of us cannot visit and a legend that has joined the stars.

Title. The Beardcap   *Design*. Vík Prjónsdóttir
Photography. Gulli Már   *Description*. Traditional
"lambshed-hood" re-interpreted for Víkurprjón in five
different colours and two shapes – The Gentleman
and The Farmer.

Title. Wild Things   *Design.* Flavio Melchiorre
Photography. Grove   *Description.* Engravings on
bamboo iPhone case for an artist series project by Joe
Mansfield, Ken Tomita and Grove.

"Every graphics tells
a different thing about you...
The prints are often the first thing
people look at when they see you."

– Kanardo

"Graphics gives subjects a deeper meaning, a face, an attitude... Graphics makes us subconsciously happy."

- Véronique Stohrer

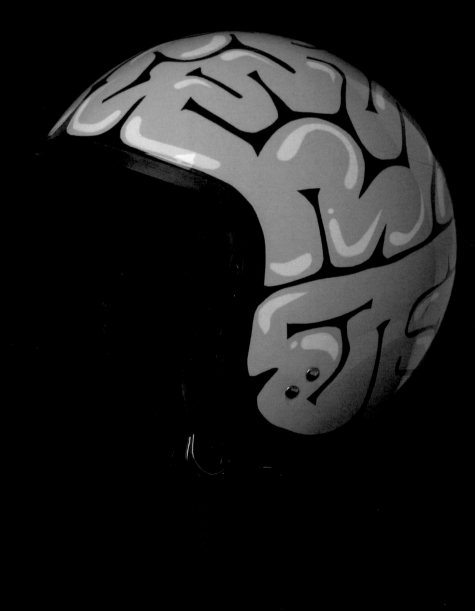

Title. Brain Box   *Design.* Death Spray Custom
Description. A crash helmet that looks like a brain
and mind as well protects your brain.

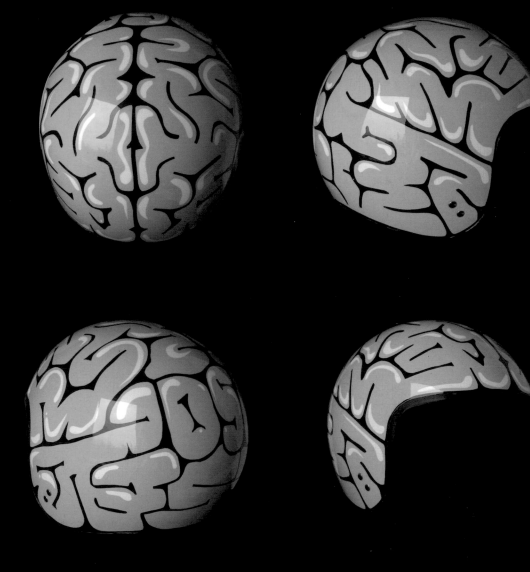

1

2

3

Title. Mini Car Wraps by TCH (on facing page) **Design.** Flavio Melchiorre **Description.** Custom car wrap design for a project initiated by The Cool Hunter.

Title. Custom Designs for Zazzle® **Design.** Flavio Melchiorre **Description.** Graphics for Keds Champion mimi slip-on sneakers and competition-shaped skateboard made of hard-rock maple.

1. Azulady   2. Dirtyviolet- 3. Flying Colours n°4

Title. De'Longhi Artista Series **Design.** Happy lovers town **Description.** Pattern for coffee machine with inspirations from children books, typography and love. Project by De'Longhi and 160 over 90.

Title. SHA-DO **Design.** Peter Buning **Description.**
Lamp shades to project patterns adjustable in size and
direction. Projections can measure up to three metres in
diameter on walls and ceiling.

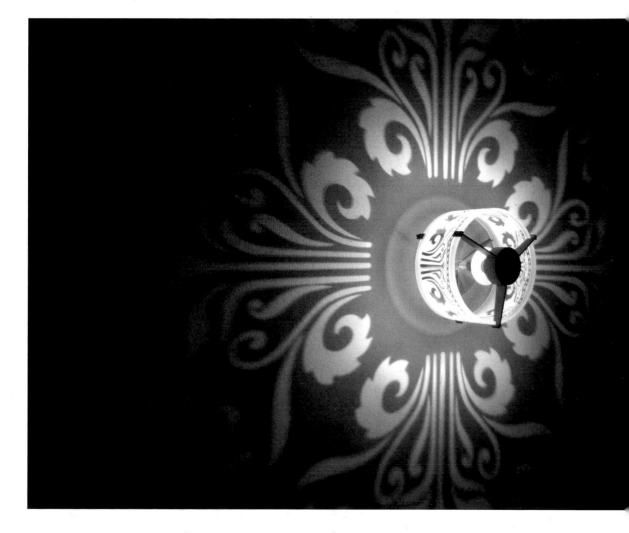

Title. SHA-DO[2] **Design.** Peter Buning
Description. Second generation of SHA-DO with lamp shades available in various colours and asymmetrical projections measuring up to one square metre in size.

"Sometimes it enchants with its uniqueness and originality and puts your imagination into a magical trip."

– Dopludó Collective

Title. Tout Va Bien   **Design.** Antoine+Manuel   **Photograph.** Rafael Vargas
Description. Cabinet for a new collection brought out by Bd Barcelona design as
a mix of arts and crafts. Comes in two versions, Basic and Top.

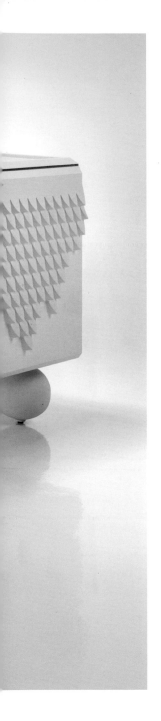
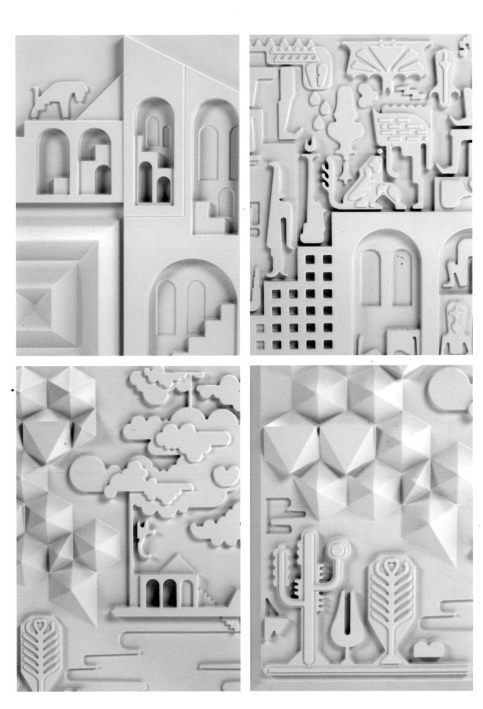

Title. Tori no Uta (Bird Song)   **Design.** Izumi Idoia
Zubia, NOMON DESIGN   **Description.** Illustration
first created for Paris music group, Izumi & Jun,
adopted in Izumi Idoia's work space and photoshooted
for Levesta's office furniture catalogue, a project of
NOMON DESIGN.

"Functional or artistic, graphic language adds another dimension to communication."

– Katrin Olina

Title. Japan / Wolf   ***Design.*** Véronique
Stohrer   ***Description.*** Photocollage for
mini-table tennis boards for I-Pong.

Title. Element   **Design.** Dizel&Sate AB
Description. Glass illustration to characterise
a consulting agency's specialties and services.

Title. MON LOU LOU   ***Design.*** Shinsuke
Koshio@SUNDAY VISION   ***Description.***
Wall illustration for a Japanese beauty salon.

Title. Lego Mojo **Design.** abgc architecture/andróid design **Photography.** studioseventyseven **Description.** Boardroom table constructed for Boys and Girls Advertising Agency. With 22,742 Lego bricks and no glue.

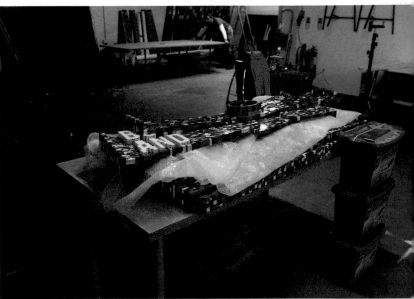

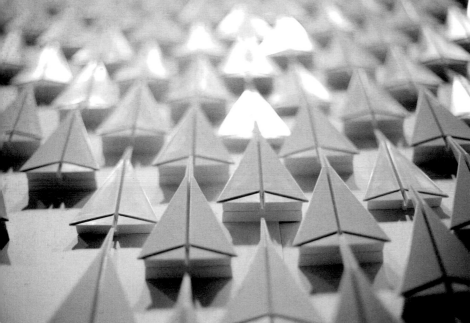

Title. Virgin Holidays Departure Lounge **Design.**
Hawaii Design **Description.** Installation engineered
out of moulded paper aeroplanes for the new Virgin
Holidays departure lounge at Gatwick Airport.

"Graphics enhance the scale of space but they cannot exist by itself. If architects are more careful with that, graphics can take a more important part of space design."

— Teradadesign Architects

Title. VilaSofa **Design.** Tjep. **Description.**
Retail design suggesting a magical vila with
moveable cash registers for a new furniture brand.

Title. Tranan **Design.** Vår, Albert France-Lanord **Description.** Seven colour mosaic artwork for the restrooms of a restaurant with a strong musical tradition in Stockholm.

Title. Flower Power Your Room **Design.**
Sarah Illenberger, Jung von Matt AG (Stuttgart)
Description. Life-sized pop-up paper installation
for air freshener brand, Ambi-Pur.

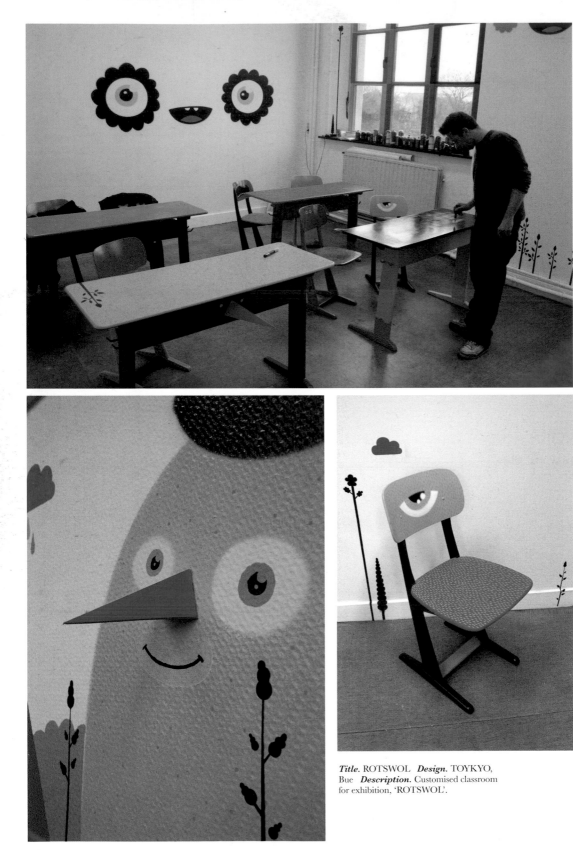

Title. ROTSWOL   ***Design***. TOYKYO,
Bue   ***Description***. Customised classroom
for exhibition, 'ROTSWOL'.

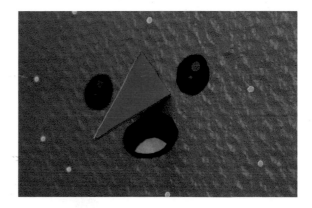

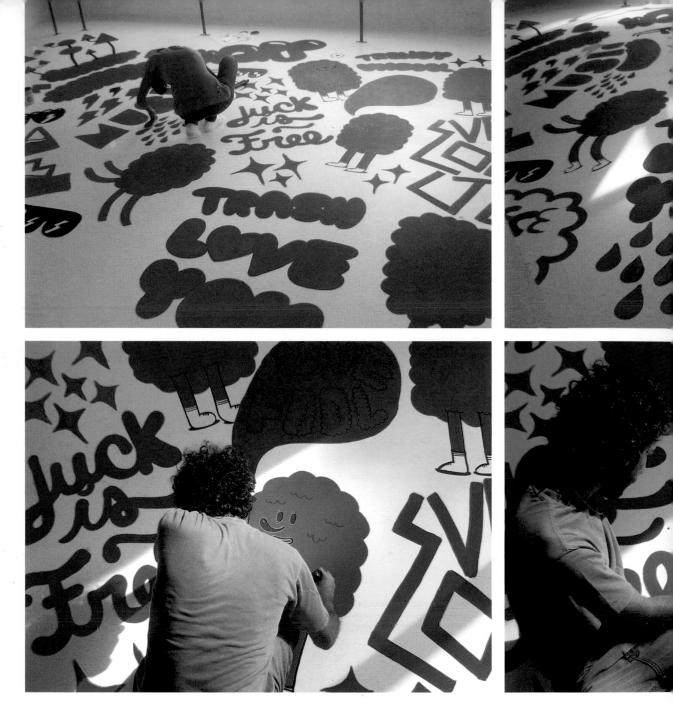

Title. Oda *Design*. Bosque studio
Description. Decoration for a boutique.

"Graphics store memories. Viewing the illustrations of your favorite childhood book might take you back to a feeling or a time."

– KnittaPlease

Title. Moominvalley – Cafeteria **Design**. Maria Yasko
Description. Space design for a family entertainment centre based on "Dangerous Summer" of the Moomin series by Finnish novelist, Tove Jansson.

Title. Moominvalley – Recreation Area
Design. Maria Yasko ***Description.*** Space
design for a family entertainment centre based
on "Moomin and the Comet" of the Moomin
series by Finnish novelist, Tove Jansson.

Title. Moominvalley – Children's Play Hall
Design. Maria Yasko *Description.* Space
design for a family entertainment centre based
on "Winter Magic" of the Moomin series by
Finnish novelist, Tove Jansson.

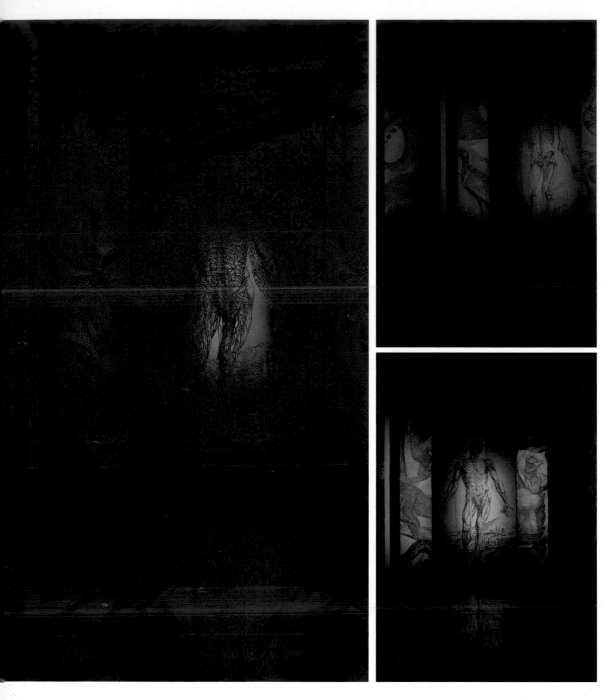

Title. RGB *Design*. carnovsky *Photography*. Luca
Volpe - *Description*. Wallpaper in three layers of motifs
corresponding with colour lights. On display at Jannelli
& Volpi store during Milan Design Week.

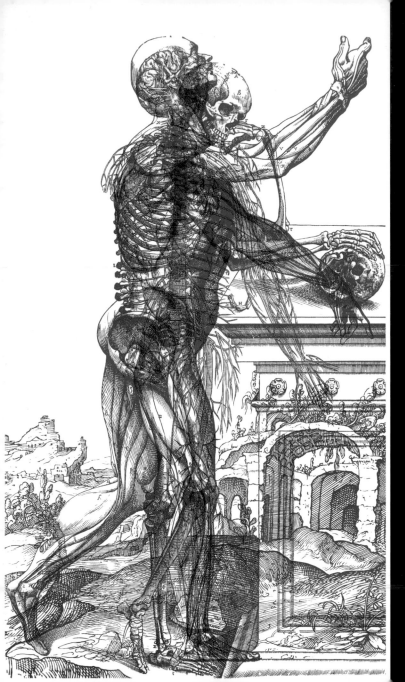
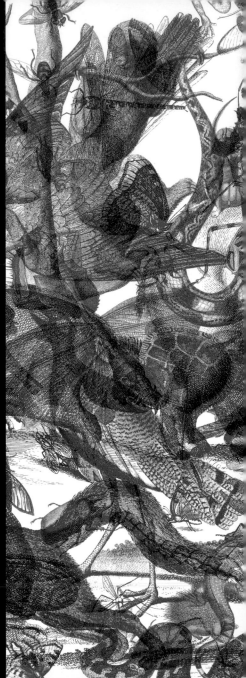

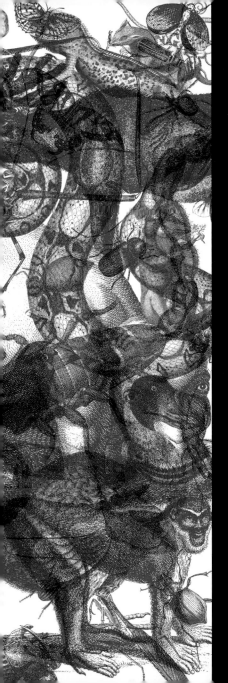
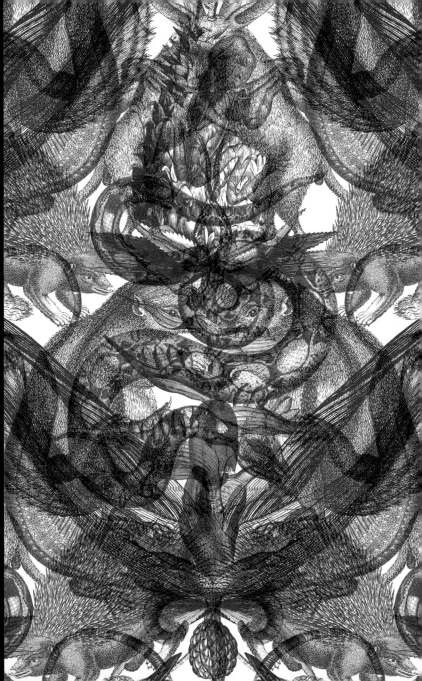

Title. Space Titled Love **Design.** Studio Lee Jang Sub, Lee Hyo Sub **Description.** Paper doll installation for an exhibition to invite children to experience emotions of love and complete the work with their own hands.

Title. Paper Garden **Design.** Studio Lee Jang
Sub **Photography.** Sin **Description.** Papercutting
installation to extend the lifespan of paper excessively
produced during printing process.

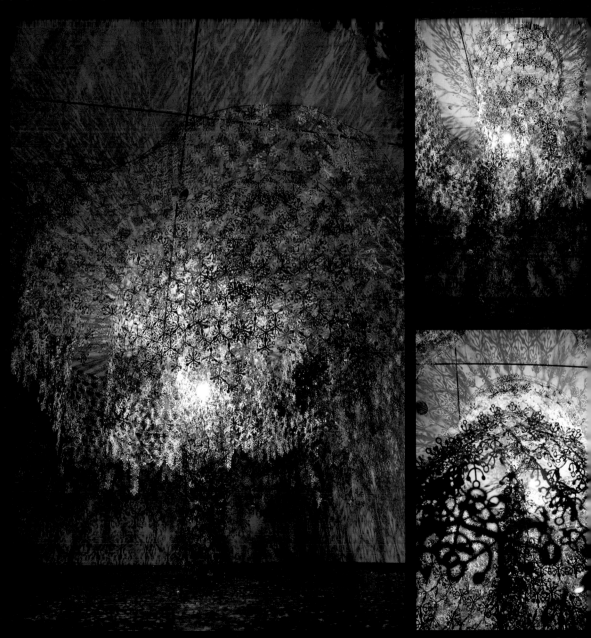

"Things in the world tattoo themselves with graphics in order to tell us their stories or how they would best like to be used."

- Peter and Sally Nencini

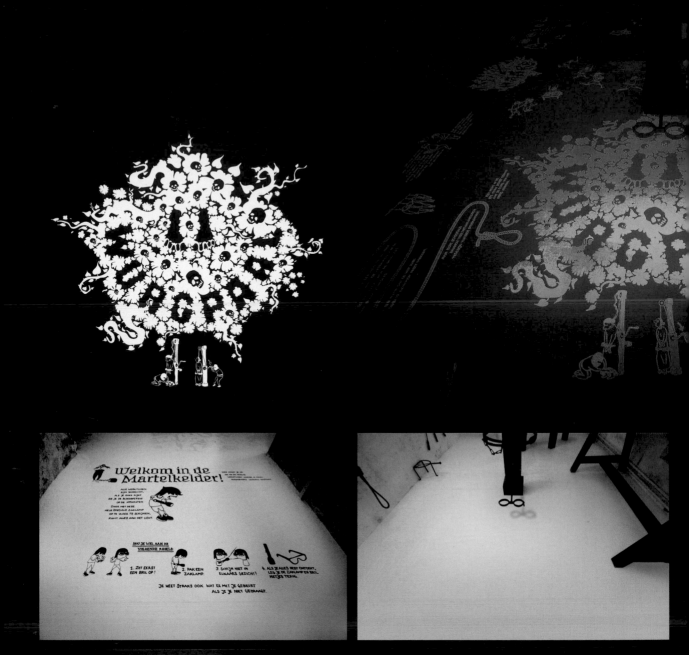

Title. The Torture Basement   ***Design.*** Trapped in Suburbia   ***Description.*** Redesign for an exhibition by Museum Gouda in a cellar, with information handrawn on the floor with UV-paint.

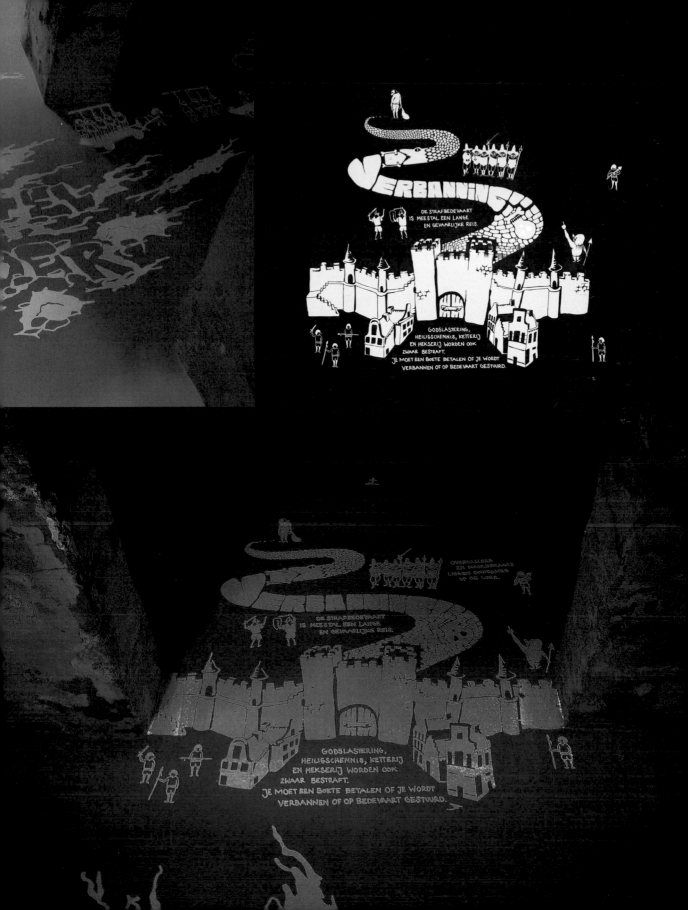

Title. PUMA Disc Blaze 90
Design. Purple Haze Studio
Description. POS/POP
materials and retail graphics
for a revitalised sneaker
design originally born in the
early 1990s.

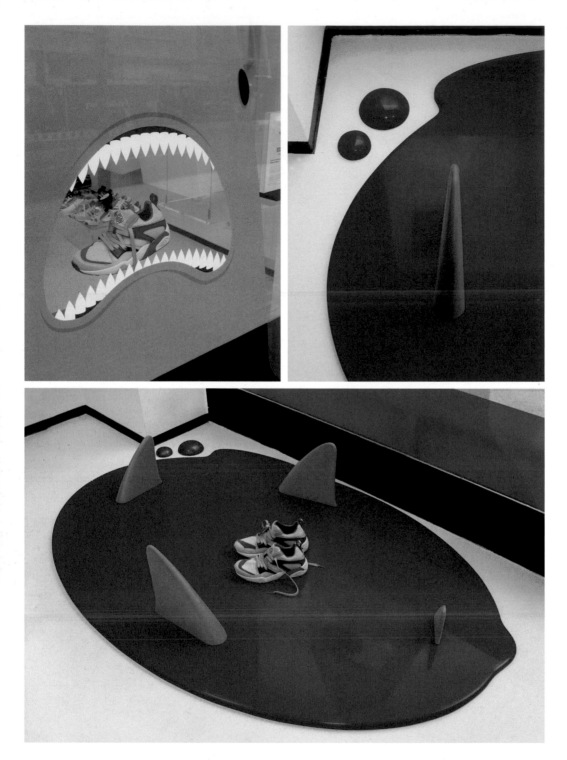

Title. PUMA x SNEAKERFREAKER **Design.**
Purple Haze Studio **Description.** POS/POP materials
and retail graphics for the Germany launch of limited
edition Blaze of Glory, a collaboration between PUMA
and Sneaker Freaker Magazine.

Title. A Yellow Rabbit in the Kaleidoscope
Eyes **Design.** Esther Lee **Description.**
Graphics display for a complex-space shared
by a café, gallery and shop at Korea Design
Foundation (KDF).

Title. Nike Lunarglide *Design*. Kustaa Saksi Ltd.
Description. Teaser campaign on the theme of
"Differences Between Men And Women" for Nike.

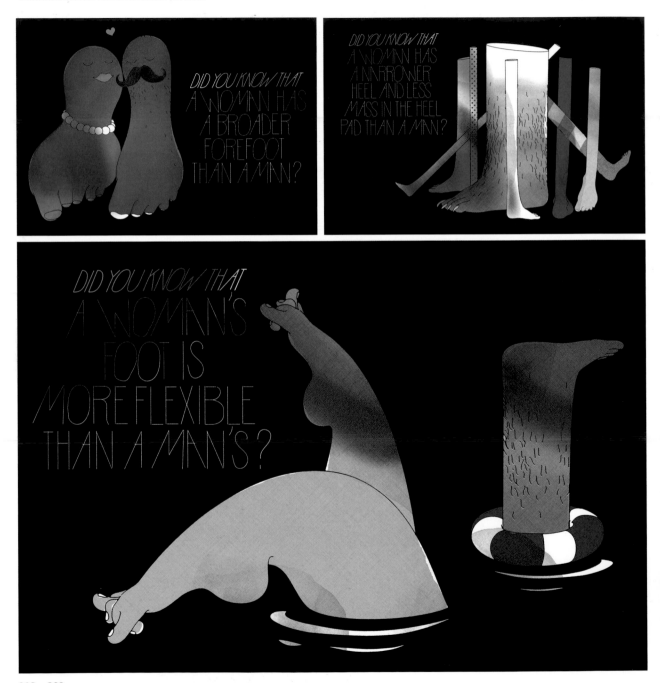

Title. Nike Running   **Design.** Kustaa Saksi Ltd.,
Nike   **Description.** Installation telling the history
and development of Nike Running at showroom
1948 in Shoreditch, London.

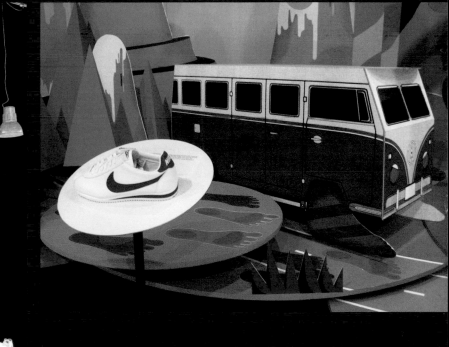

"Graphics is a tool to relate its physical products more personally and directly to a wide variety of people with different tastes, love, interests and needs."

– Vitamin

Title. Detail 1, 2, 3   ***Design.*** Staynice, Loulou, Tummie
Description. Handpainted graphics for Playgrounds Festival
completed in 2009 to celebrate motion, animation and
characters in Tilburg, the Netherlands.

Title. Cafeteria / La Biennale di Venezia   ***Artwork.***
Tobias Rehberger ***Furniture.*** Artek ***Description.***
Visually disorienting environment realised for the
cafeteria of Palazzo delle Exposizioni della Biennale,
referencing specific examples of Dazzle camouflage.

Photography. Katja Hagelstam

Photography. Wolfgang Guenzel

Photography. Wolfgang Guenzel

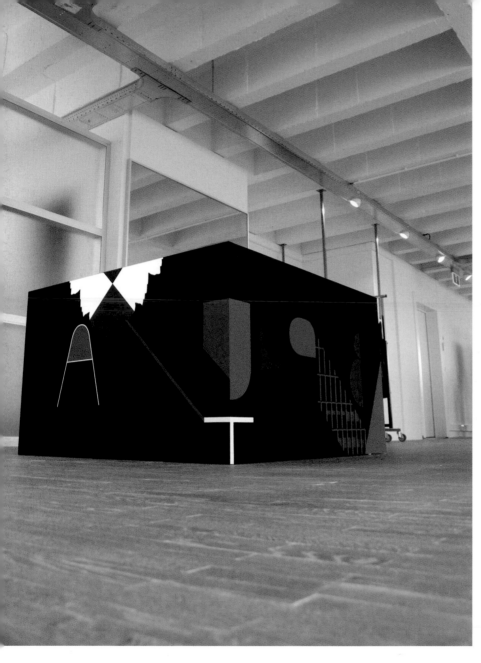

Title. New City, New Nature **Design**. Staynice
Description. Collage artwork mixing urban and
organic elements to create 'New Nature, New City',
theme of Van Gils' 2010 collection.

Title. Wandarbeit Nr. 16 (on facing page, top)
Installation. Esther Stocker ***Description.*** Masking tape
installation for exhibition "Ob ich das sehe (whether I see
that)" at Heidelberger Kunstverein in Heidelberg, Germany.
Courtesy of Galerie Krobath Wimmer, Vienna.

Title. What I Don't Know About Space (on facing page,
bottom) ***Installation.*** Esther Stocker ***Photography.***
Andy Keates ***Description.*** Masking tape, foam core and
emulsion paint installation for exhibition "What I Don't
Know About Space" at MUSEUM 52 in London, UK.

Title. Abstract Thought Is A Warm Puppy
Installation. Esther Stocker ***Photography.*** Sacha
Georg ***Description.*** Wood and emulsion paint
installation for exhibition "Abstract Thought Is A Warm
Puppy" at Center for Contemporary Non-Objective
Art in Brussels, Belgium. Courtesy of Galerie Krobath
Wimmer, Vienna.

"Basically everything is graphics... what really fascinates me is the way of it being elusive, with its beauty lays on its ambiguity."

- carnovsky

Title. Illoiha Omotesando   **Design.** nendo
Description. Rock-climbing wall installation
blending Tokyo's fashion district elements with
intensive sports as the fitness club suggests
– "Becoming beautiful through movement".

Title. Moss House   ***Design.*** nendo   ***Description.***
Pattern composed of dry moss to connect the old wooden
house interior to the riverside moss outside the house.

Title. paramodelic – graffiti
Design. Paramodel
Description. Installation art for "kita!! Japanese Artist Meets Indonesia". Courtesy of Mori Yu Gallery.

Title. Cherbourg Primary School
Design. SHH   **Description.** Graphics
to add a sense of nature, colour and
character to the multi-functional space
of a primary school. Commissioned
by The School Food Trust.

"Graphics conveys ideas, and ideas have the potential to inspire, provoke, interrupt and assist in our daily lives."

– YesYesNo

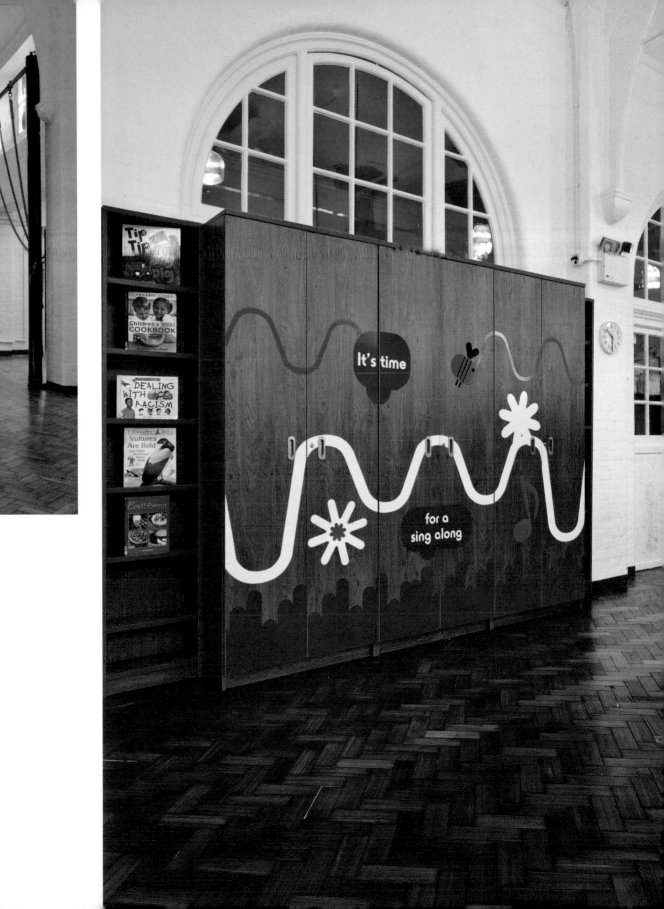

Title. Applemore College *Design.*
SHH *Description.* Graphics inspired
by new steel beams to create a semi-
industrial environment for the school's
cafeteria. Commissioned by The
School Food Trust.

Title. Senzoku Gakuen College of Music –
The Black Hall *Design*. TERADADESIGN
ARCHITECTS *Description*. Interior and
signage system design for a new rock and pop
music school, The Black Hall.

Title. Panos 2013 *Planning & curation.*
Kanardo *Description.* Second edition of
Panos, project for Arty Farty at Ville de Lyon,
featuring fake street signs by 52 artists invited
from around the world.

1. Stereotype 2. :Phunk Studio 3. Skooly DK
4. Meomi 5. Boris Hoppek 6. Martin Krusche
7. Superdeux 8. Steven Harrington 9. Superdeux

9

10

Title. Panos 2013
Planning & Curation *Kozyndan*

1. Kozyndan   2. Delarocca   3. Benjamin Güedel
4. DEVILROBOTS   5. Mike Perry   6. Cody
Hudson   7. Emil Kozak   8. Jeremyville
9. Easy Hey   10. 123klan   11. iLK

11

Title. W+K window gallery **Design.** Driv Loo
Description. Illustrations and vinyl stickers for
Wieden+Kennedy Shanghai window panels based
on the theme – Underground.

Title. Bookbus **Design.** Muungano, Fredrik Forsberg@TheyGraphics **Photography.** Clive Tompsett **Description.** Interior and exterior graphics for a mobile library of Kiruna City Library.

Title. Fantastic Gymnastic **Design.** MessyMsxi **Description.** Painting commissioned by Singapore Post to promote mailbox painting project, STAMP 02. Characters were inspired by the box's locality and responding to the Youth Olympic Games to be held in Singapore.

Title. Untitled **Design.** KnittaPlease **Photography.**
Fabrizio Ribechi **Description.** Knit graffiti on urban
features for exhibition "Dritto Rovescio (Craft Turned On
Its Head)". Commissioned by Triennale Design Museum.

Title. Mexico City bus **Design.** KnittaPlease
Photography. Cesar Ortega **Description.** Knit graffiti
on a city bus for Gallery Elaboratorio. A project sponsored
by Absolut Volka.

Title. MOSAIC in Beijing **Design.** SAKO Architects / Keiichiro SAKO **Photography.** Shu He, Misae Hiromatsu@BEIJING NDC STUDIO, INC. **Description.** Architectural and interior design for a Beijing residential and commercial development project. Commissioned by Beijing Guo Rong Real Estate Development Ltd.

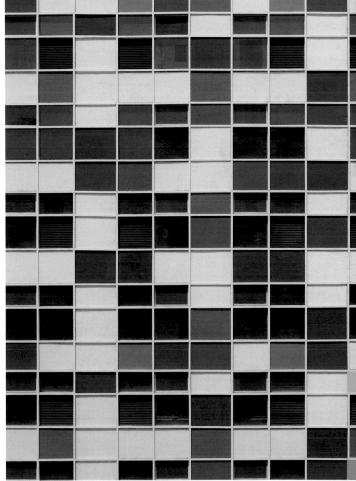

Title. MOSAIC in Beijing **Design.** SAKO Architects
/ Keiichiro SAKO **Photography.** Shu He, Misae
Hiromatsu@BEIJING NDC STUDIO, INC.

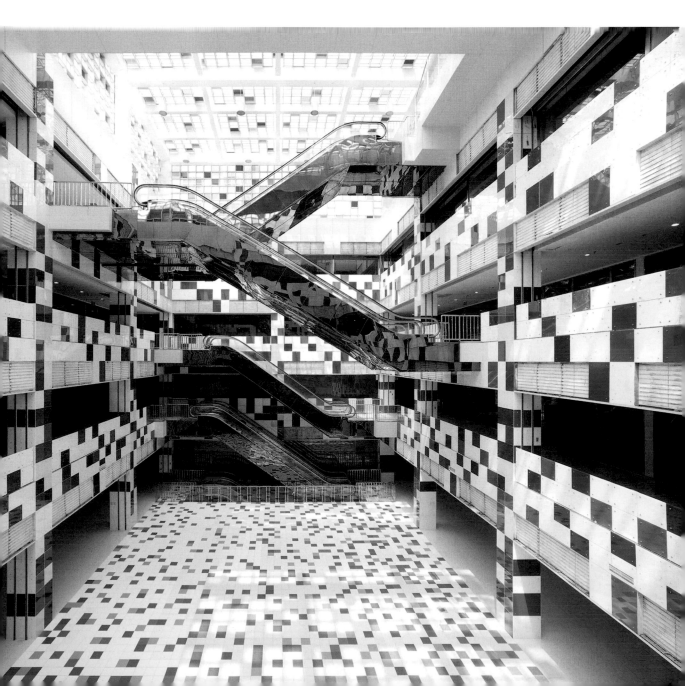

Title. Obsessions Make My Life Worse And My Work Better   *Design.* Sagmeister Inc.   *Photography.* Jens Rehr   *Description.* Euro cents installation at Waagdragerhof Square in Amsterdam for Droog Event 2: Urban Play.

better and my work better

"We can be blind to some of them and some of them make us stop and think. Graphics can scare and heal."

- Kristina Sabaite

Title. Night Lights **Design.** YesYesNo **Description.**
Interactive installation for NZ Telecom, realised with The
Church, Inside Out Productions and Electric Canvas.

Title. Night Lights *Design.* YesYesNo

Know-who
biography

3Min. Graphic Associates & Duomo Co., Ltd

Specialising in graphic design, Tokyo-based 3MIN. works with DUOMO CO.,LTD in Kyoto for the production of *KYO-TO-TO*, an embroidery brand as a mix of the traditional and contemporary centers of Japan. DUOMO undertakes the embroidery work and 3MIN. is responsible for the graphics and design.

abgc architecture/ andróid design

abgc architecture/andróid design is Andrew Brady and Gearóid Carvill, graduates of the School of Architecture of University College Dublin. The practice operates through collaborative process involving crafts, people, artists and other creatives in the field of furniture, exhibition and theatre design, as well as residential and commercial design out of South Studios in Dublin's historic Blackpitts area. Brady is an enthusiastic furniture maker and Carvill an obsessive salad gardener when at home.

Alexander Girard

The Estate of Alexander Girard is officially represented by máXimo. Girard has once led the Herman Miller textile division and re-designed the Braniff Airlines, the La Fonda del Sol Restaurant in New York and the Textiles&Objects shop in the 1960s. Girard used traditional folk art to infuse colour, whimsy and humor into modern design. máXimo has partnered with the Girard family to bring his extensive body of work into the contemporary market through collaborations with design oriented companies including Herman Miller, Maharam, Vitra, Kate Spade, Chronicle Books and House Industries.

Angus & Celeste

Angus & Celeste designs an exquisite range of handmade porcelain jewellery, accessories and homewares. The Australian duo draws inspiration by combining old world engravings with their own illustrations and photographs of the natural world. They have developed a 'home-baked' aesthetic theory with their own craftspeople in Australia.

Anne Marie Skjoldager Jensen

Born in Aarhus, Denmark, in 1981, Skjoldager Jensen studied fashion at the Danish Design School (DKDS) in Copenhagen and later moved to Paris to study at the Ecole Nationale Superieure des Arts Decoratifs before her internship at Bernhard Wilhelm's atelier and John Galliano's studio. The Danish designer was a finalist in fashion competition, Createurope 2009 in Berlin, where she showed her collection *One eye laughing, the other crying*. She currently works at Balenciaga.

Antoine+Manuel

Antoine Audiau and Manuel Warosz met in an art school in Paris and shortly decided to work together under the name Antoine+Manuel in 1993. The French duo has defined a unique graphic style by combining handdrawings and computer illustration with their own typography and photography in fields ranging from dance to fashion via contemporary art and design. Their clients include *Christian Lacroix, Habitat, Galeries Lafayette, Domestic* and *Larousse*.

Arbito

Arbito's art tells the visual tale of a ragtag band of hippie vagabonds on a pop-psychedelic trip. His resin figures have been shown to the world in solo and group shows, and also at Phillips de Pury Auction and Art Basel. He shares a studio in the Pacific Northwest with The Hobo, Seeker, Sammy, Patty Power and his wife, Snaggs.

Artek

Building on the design heritage of Alvar Aalto, Artek is one of the most innovative contributors to modern design since 1935. Combining 'art' and 'technology', Artek's furniture can be found in various types of spaces, from public spaces to homes, museums to schools and hotels to offices.

Bas van de Poel & Daan van Dam

Bas van de Poel and Daan van Dam is an Amsterdam-based creative team who study advertising at the Willem de Kooning Academy in Rotterdam. Both of them share a passion for the different and the unknown. During the weekend, they kick back with a few good Sci-fi novels and seventies porn flicks.

Bosque studio

Bosque is the fusion of four graphic designers and artists formed in 2008 in Buenos Aires, Argentina. The creative studio finds its inspiration from music, art, illustrations, film, photography and daily life. Their speciality includes corporate identity, editorial design, illustration, installation, photography and productions for the fashion industry.

Brendan Lee Satish Tang

Brendan Lee Satish Tang is a naturalised Canada citizen born to Trinidadian parents in Dublin, Ireland. Tang has exhibited his work in juried and invitational shows at the Vancouver Art Gallery, as well as Ottawa Art Gallery and Kentucky Museum of Art and Craft. He currently resides in Kamloops, British Columbia.

carnovsky

carnovsky is Milan-based design studio comprised of Francesco Rugi and Silvia Quintanilla.

Coco Studio

As an illustrator, Coco's background gives her a unique insight into fashion and art. She has worked as a communication consultant for a number of leading fashion designers after spending five years studying fine arts in Paris, and later moved to London and set up a creative and technology consultancy, getConfused, in 2004. Coco loves the results of mixing techniques while also aiming for restraints and minimalism in the finished work.

David Carvalho

Born in 1980, David Carvalho is Portuguese-born artist and designer who has been developing work in many design disciplines, including the launch of his first design-related PDF magazine, *Camouflage*; and the establishment of his own practice, Pkage Design, and online design store, Propaganda, with designer friend, Nuno Salvaterra in 2003 and 2004. Carvalho was also the founder and fashion editor of online lifestyle magazine, *Rua de B*. Carvalho is currently a senior designer at View.

Death Spray Custom
P. 138-139

Death Spray Custom was formed in London in 2008. With no agenda other than to celebrate uniquness, Death Spray Custom combines elements of Californian custom culture, European aesthetic and simple ideas for unique and genre-crossing results.

Dizel & Sate AB
P. 156-157

Dizel&Sate is a Stockholm-based Swedish design studio that has long been active with alternative architecture, challenging traditional conceptions of minimalism and functionality. Their portfolio includes commissioned design of both retail and office spaces, alongside installations for public venues, with single illustrations or complete graphic profiles.

Dopludó Collective
Cover illustrations, P. 076-081

Dopludó is the French phonetic transcription of 'deux plus deux', which literally means 'two plus two' in English and, at the heart of the name of the creative trio, lays the absurd mathematical formula "2+2=5'. Dopludó Collective was found in St. Petersburg in 2006. Together they work with images from magic fairy tales, folk elements and more or less abstract content on installations, objects, illustrations, interiors and public projects in cold Russia and Scandinavia.

Dorophy Tang
P. 082-085

Dorophy Tang is a Hong Kong-based graphic designer and illustrator best known for her Qinghuaqi fusion art. Tang's art has been featured in the Beijing Olympics and Paralympic Games. The artist holds a degree in industrial and product design from Hong Kong Polytechnic University.

Surprise!

Driv Loo
P. 242-243

Born in Malaysia in 1983, DrivLoo is drawn to design, illustration, typography and stupid ideas at all times. He currently works and lives in Shanghai.

Esther Lee
P. 206-207

Esther Lee is an illustrator and graphic designer born and based in Seoul, Korea. Lee has studied advertising communication design at Hongik University and graduated in 2006.

Esther Stocker
P. 222-223

Italian-born Esther Stocker received her education at Akademie der Bildenden Künste in Vienna, Accademia di Belle Arti di Brera in Milano and Art Center College of Design in Pasadena, California. Besides her master tape installation, Stocker also produces paintings and photography works. She is the recipient of *Preis der Stadt Wien* in 2009.

Fehling & Peiz
P. 090-091

Yvonne Fehling and Jennie Peiz are both product design graduates of Staatliche Hochschule für Gestaltung Karlsruhe (University of Media Arts and Design) and assistant professor at the University of Karlsruhe in Germany. The duo founded their design studio and brand *Kraud* in 2006.

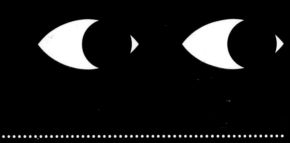

Flavio Melchiorre

After ten years of experience in typography, advertising and fashion, Italian-born Flavio Melchiorre has developed his personal style with inspirations from life, people and places he visited, bringing art to life by combining free-hand drawings with chromatic and iconographic effects. From single drawings to the many different digital elaborations derived, Melchiorre's work presents endless, potential evolutions.

Frédérique Morrel

Witnessing how her grandmother spent long evenings making giant beautiful needlework canvas which eventually went into trash bins after her death, Frédérique Morrel starts redeeming vintage tapestries as a tribute to the dedicated work of these anonymous women. With an enormous collection of vintage artifacts, Morrel composes emotional tales that speak about transmission between styles, generations, historical periods.

Thinking
minus
language
...

Hanna Melin

Born in Sweden, 1978, Hanna Melin moved to England in 1998 to study art, including a bachelor's degree in illustration in Brighton University and an MA in Communication from the Royal College of Art. Melin now lives and works as an illustrator and artist in the east end of London.

Happy lovers town

Born in Pistoia, Italy, Jonathan Calugi is an illustrator with each of his pieces being a take on his quirky child-like doodles with clean minimal lines and simple colours. And it is how Calugi draws viewers to a basic stand and cultivates appreciation of the very epitome of 'Less is more'.

Hawaii Design

Established by Paul McAnelly in 2005, Hawaii prides itself in being more than just a design agency in London. Notable for its originality, diversity and transparent working methodology, Hawaii offers diverse creative services, including identity and exhibition design. The agency was recently shortlisted for the Brit Insurance *Design Of The Year Award*.

Heal fashion lab.

French couple Alice Reydellet and Hervé Koelich met each other about a decade ago and began their partnership under the composite name, Heal, after their fabric design jobs for Christian Lacroix haute couture. Heal is a luxury ready-to-wear brand recognised by its bold palettes splashed onto architectural silhouettes.

Heather Lins Home

Founded in 2008, Heather Lins Home integrates modern design, artisan production techniques and eco-friendly materials into artful textiles for homes. Lins is a graphic designer who finds her inspiration while examining and re-imagining the ordinary in life.

Héctor Serrano Studio

Héctor Serrano Studio is founded by Héctor Serrano in 2000. Combining innovation with the communication of familiar ideas in areas of product, space and visual communication design, the office has won various awards, like the *Peugeot Design Award* and *Designer of the year 2009* by AD magazine. Serrano studied industrial design in Valencia before he obtained his Master's degree in product design at The Royal College of Art.

Irana Douer

P. 070-071

Irana Douer is an art student at IUNA university and freelance artist in Buenos Aires, Argentina, where she was born. Douer is also the founder and curator of *Ruby Mag*, a monthly-based online art magazine.

Izumi Idoia Zubia

P. 152-153

French-and-Spanish-born Izumi Idoia Zubia has been a freelance illustrator in Paris since 2006. Upon her completion of studies in architecture, multimedia arts and lyrical music, she moved to Barcelona and spent six years to work in Dresslab, NomonDesign, FlightTag, Agatha Ruiz De La Prada, Jordi Labanda, etc. as web graphic designer and illustrator. Zubia specialises in fashion illustration, textile prints, magazines, children books and flash animations.

Kanardo

P. 046-047, 238-241

Kanardo is a two-headed Guethary-based unit specialising in art direction and graphic design for board culture brands. Their portfolio includes branding and identity, art direction and layout for magazines, curation for exhibitions and books, contemporary photography and illustrations for a various range of printed brochures and clothing.

Katrin Olina

P. 170-173

Icelandic designer and artist Katrin Olina's quasi-narrative graphic language reflects her own inner landscape – a fantastical world that is supernatural, organic and dreamlike at once. Born in Iceland, Olina studied industrial design at the E.S.D.I. in Paris before getting her feet wet in the design studios of Philippe Starck in Paris and Ross Lovegrove in London. Her signature products include silk scarves and handpainted porcelain products, as well as a vinyl collectible toy collection created in 2007.

Keren Richter

P. 058-061

Keren Richter is a Brooklyn-based visual artist specialising in illustration and art direction. Her psychedelic landscapes and stylish portraits have found their way into a variety of projects and signature products for clients like MTV, Nylon, Vans, Sephora and Urban Outfitters. Most recently, Richter has begun curating. Her first magazine project, *Space is the Place*, came out in summer 2010.

Kim Joon

P. 108-111

Born in Seoul, 1966, Kim Joon explores the beauty of body and tattoo art via the medium of digital print. Joon is currently a professor at the Department of Cartoon and Animation of Kongju National University. He holds a BA in painting from Hongik University and an MA in painting from Hongik University in Seoul, Korea.

Kiyoshi Kuroda

P. 072-073

Born in Tokyo, 1975, Kiyoshi Kuroda has started his career as an illustrator and art director since 2003 after his graduation from Tama Art University. He has received *Good Design Award* for his wall graphic through Shinjuku Southern Beat Project, and is a visiting professor at Osaka Seikei University.

KnittaPlease

P. 248-249

Magda Sayeg began KnittaPlease in 2005 in response to the disappearing human qualities in urban environment, and by inserting handmade art in a landscape of concrete and steel, she adds warmth back to the streets with traditional crafts and unused materials. KnittaPlease represents the pleasant energy coming from knitting and more extensively weaving, while giving a nod to its powerful history. Sayeg is currently based in Austin, Texas.

Kristina Sabaite

Lithuanian-born Kristina Sabaite is a children's book illustrator and graphic designer based in the north of Spain. Her projects feature a collection of beautiful handmade things derived from the artist's own illustration work.

Kustaa Saksi Ltd.

Kustaa Saksi's illustrations are a syrupy disarray of playful, paradoxical and often over-glossy elements which are also inviting, troubling, messy, and yet strangely clear. The Finnish-born illustrator currently resides in Paris and is missioned to combine viscous shapes with organic touches to create a new world psychedelia.

Design makes me happy!

Maria Yasko

Twenty-four-year-old Maria Yasko is born in the Komi Republic and currently resides in Moscow. Upon her graduation from the Moscow College of Humanities and Economics and the Moscow Humanitarian-Economic Institute, Yasko takes up the job as an interior and industrial designer at Marisko Studio. Yasko's work often draws attention to the forms of plants and the animal world so as to engage the audience with their roots in nature.

Lifelounge

With over 11 years of dedication in the digital arena, Lifelounge Group always strives to live life from a different angle and create pure awesomeness in everything they do.

Malotaprojects

Mar Hernández aka Malota is an interdisciplinary artist graduated with a BA in fine arts. She develops a wide and varied interests in the field of music, illustration, design and art for international clients including Armada skis (USA), Cactus Island Recordings (UK), Revista Colectiva (Costa Rica) , d[x]i magazine (Spain) and argh comic (Spain).

MessyMsxi

Hailed from the little island of Singapore, Msxi has learnt to find beauty in the vernacular and had dreams of a bigger world and a brighter everyday. Msxi has been exploring unique concepts and themes via illustrations in various media to review her personal experiences and subjects that interest her at most. She is currently pursuing her studies in illustraions at Central Saint Martins, London on government scholarship.

Mottoform

Mottoform is a Helsinki-based design studio specialising in product, furniture, interior and graphics. Established by Elizabeth Salonen in 2005, the studio aims to inspire by introducing fresh perspectives and flexible approaches in constructing stories in new products. Salonen is of Canada origin and has studied design in Finland and the United States. She holds a degree in industrial design from the College for Creative Studies in Detroit, Michigan, USA.

Muungano

Muungano is a Swedish design group established in 1996. Through its projects, the group has been consciously finding challenges and motivation in pushing the boundaries of the brief, by contextualising problems and assuming a holistic approach. Muungano means 'fusion' or 'unification' in Swahili. The name is adopted to honour the goals, activities and business of Muungano.

nendo

nendo is a design firm founded by architect Oki Sato in Tokyo in 2002. The firm holds the goal of bringing small surprises to people through multidisciplinary practices of different media including architecture, interiors, furniture, industrial products and graphic design.

Paramodel

Paramodel is Yasuhiko Hayashi (b. 1971) and Yusuke Nakano (b. 1976) who have teamed up to work since 2001. The work they produced are named 'Paradise model' which contains a variety of expression techniques and media such as animation, painting, the solid, photograph and sake. They are both graduates of Kyoto City University of Arts.

Peter & Sally Nencini

Peter and Sally Nencini met at the Royal College of Art. Collectively, they source and rework chairs, extracting a narrative out of its past for its prospective user. Individually, they have designed for clients including Levi's, BBC, Channel 4 and ITV.

Peter Buning

Born in 1973 in Germany, Peter Buning has been freelancing since 1995 and working in Atelier5, an open workspace for art and design in Bocholt since 2005. Buning explored light and media techniques while he's involved in projects of 3deluxe, and began to emphasise light and shadow effects in his lighting design in 2001. His lamps were presented at exhibitions held in Cologne, Frankfurt, Düsseldorf, etc.

Purple Haze Studio

Purple Haze is a multidisciplinary graphic design studio based in Munich, Germany. The unit produces intelligent and progressive communication solutions for print or packaging, brand applications, publishing, exhibitions and websites for national and international projects which involve conception, art direction, typography, design and illustration skills.

Sagmeister Inc.

Stefan Sagmeister formed Sagmeister Inc. in 1993. A five-time Grammies nominee and winner of many important international design awards, the native Austrian obtained his MFA from the University of Applied Arts in Vienna and, as a Fulbright Scholar, a Master's degree from Pratt Institute in New York. His work has been published in the book, *Things I Have Learned in My Life So Far*, by Abrams. Sagmeister currently teaches in the graduate department of the School of Visual Art in New York.

Sako Architects / Keiichiro Sako

Experienced in residential and commercial designs so as public services facilities such as government buildings and museums, SAKO Architects' expertise encompassses a wide range of disciplines, from architecture and interior design, to urban planning, furniture, landscape and graphic design. SAKO's interior design has been approved by the *JCD Design Award* for more than five successive years and design awards in China.

Sarah Illenberger

Defining one category for all the work of Sarah Illenberger is no easy task. The forms the visual translations of her themes assume are far too diverse. Illenberger's creations meticulous handworks, incorporating the most mundane materials at times. Illenberger has started her practice in Berlin since 2007. She was trained to be a designer at Chelsea College and Central Saint Martins.

SHH

SHH is an architectural practice and interior and branding design consultancy founded by David Spence, Graham Harris and Neil Hogan in 1992. With a highly international workforce and portfolio, the company initially made its name in ultra-high-end residential schemes before extending its expertise to include leisure, workspace and retail schemes. SHH's leisure portfolio includes the award-winning McDonald's Oxford Street flagship restaurant and the Michelin-starred The Greenhouse.

Snaggs

Snaggs' artist career was inspired by stuffed Nauga Monsters from the 1960s. Her rainbow-coloured body of work has a retro modern style that combines the handmade quality of craft with the sensibility of clean design. Snaggs' felt and vinyl crafts has recently shown in Australia, Hong Kong, New York and Los Angeles and honourably displayed alongside Andy Warhol's and Shepard Fairy's works in the Christies, Pop Culture Auction in 2009.

Staynice

Staynice is the van Dijck brothers, Rob and Barry, who started their company in 2007 after graduating from AKV St. Joost's Academy of Fine Arts, in Breda, the Netherlands. The brothers find their roots in the graffiti and street-art movement which is directly shown in the unadjusted way. They focus their business on printed matter but would also do handpaint graphics on walls.

Studio Kluif

Studio Kluif is set up by Jeroen Hoedjes and Paul Roeters in 1999. Currently, Kluif has grown to a team of ten designers from home or abroad. Without losing sight of the original core values on simplicity, humour and putting things into perspective, Studio Kluif has developed into a fully fledged and multifaceted design studio. Kluif's work has been published in two books, *Purists are boring* and Pacifist punks.

Studio Lee Jang Sub

Lee Jang Sub was born and raised in Korea, and is currently working in Seoul. Lee believes that complexity does not necessarily indicate uneasiness and disorder but rich aesthetic possibility and creative energy. He has been experimenting with this idea in various media.

Studio Lisa Bengtsson

Lisa Bengtsson opened her company after she completed her studies at Berghs School of Communication in Stockholm, Sweden in 2007. Bengtsson creates pattern and illustrations for almost anything that comes in her way and her biggest inspiration has been people, their behaviors and the way they live or used to live. She is always trying to find a way to insert her own values and thoughts into her projects and designs.

Studio Violet

Camilla Engman and Elisabeth Dunker have joined hands to set up Studio Violet in 2008. Both Engman and Dunker received their education at HDK in Gothenburg. The two have, however, decided to close the studio in 2010.

traditional graffiti and become a well-known name in the international streetart scene. 'TABAS' is the derivation of a French slang expression, "Ça tabasse!", which means "It bits up!"

Teradadesign Architects
P. 236-237

Established in 2003, TERADADESIGN offers a wide range of design oriented services in the area of architecture, interior, furniture and product designs. Its founder, Naoki Terada, studied engineering at the Meji University in Japan, and at Archietectural Association School of Architecture in London, receiving the AA Diploma in 1994.

Tjep.
P. 166-167

Brought up in Geneva, Brussels and New York, Frank Tjepkema (b. 1970) graduated from the Design Academy Eindhoven with honours in 1996. Tjepkema's work covers products, furniture, accessories, interior design and interior architecture and his portfolio includes the design for the widely acclaimed Restaurant Fabbrica in Rotterdam and Heineken's flagship-store in Amsterdam. Tjep's work can be found in the world's most influential galleries, such as Moss in New-York.

TheyGraphics
P. 244-245

TheyGraphics was formed in 2006 by Jiri Adamik-Novak and Fredrik Forsberg where both hold an MA in graphic design at Konstfack University College of Arts and Design in Stockholm The multidisciplinary studio produces design and illustration for arts, culture, books and fashion.

Toykyo
P. 028-037, 064-065, 176-177

TOYKYO is a creative agency founded in 2006 by Mathieu Van Damme and Benjamin Van Oost, who have also established the collective creative platform, TOYKYO PRODUCTIONS, as well as TOYKYO KIDS with Bue and An Oost. They represent some of the most talented contemporary graphic designers and illustrators and produce brand identities in Ghent, Belgium.

Trapped in Suburbia
P. 196-201

Trapped in Suburbia enjoys working at the edge, challenging themselves and those around them and looking further than the length of their noses. They create conceptually and strategically strong projects with clear, clever solutions and designs. They think before they act, and act before they talk. This is what they call 'smart design'.

Vår

Vår is a Stockholm-based studio made of Karl Grandin and Björn Atldax who joined forced in 1996. Atldax is an alumnus of Beckmans School of Design and Gradin is from Sandberg Institute in Amsterdam. Their illustrations often appear as a wonderland of grotesque characters in collaboration projects and *Cheap Monday* clothings, which they launched with friends in 2004.

Véronique Stohrer

Véronique Stohrer is an illustrator and designer who graduated in 2004 with a graphic design diploma at Pforzheim College of Art. Stohrer has been freelancing for various agencies and private clients and creating new perspectives in little art objects and sewed items to sell in shops. Her art is a fusion of materials, traditions and modernism and a mix of hand-drawings, vector-based illustration, photography and collage.

Vík Prjónsdóttir

Vík Prjónsdóttir is the collaboration between Brynhildur Pálsdóttir, Egill Kalevi Karlsson, Gudfinna Mjöll Magnúsdóttir, Hrafnkell Birgisson, Thurídur Rós Sigurthorsdóttir and Vikwool, one of the oldest and best-known knitwear producers in Iceland. The project was meant to revaluate the image of the Icelandic wool industry through unconventional product development. Their wool products were unique and sustainable source made from a combination of fibers and 100% Icelandic sheep wool.

Vitamin

With its product range spanning from ceramics, sports accessories and now furniture, London-based Vitamin is ready to put its own fresh spin on any product. Their latest design includes free-standing bottle openers, vases with integrated ashtrays or table lights that hopefully make their owners' lives a little less ordinary.

Vivi Dot

Vivi Dot is a collection of handmade accessories featuring bold fabric covered buttons that can be extended to become rings, hair accessories, cuff links, watch necklaces and other casual statement pieces that are guaranteed to stand out. Each original graphic is collaboratively created by Molly Gaines and Duncan Hooper.

Wahahafactory

Wahahafactory is a multimedia creation unit established in 2006 by May Sum who is constantly pushing and blurring the boundaries between painting and make-up. With vast experience in creative media along fashion, photography, art direction and print design, May Sum finds her most essential motivation for creation in the promotion of happiness and enhancement of individuality in everyone.

YesYesNo

YesYesNo is a new interactive collective specialising in the creation of engaging and magical installations that combine creativity, artistic vision and cutting edge R&D. Founded in 2008 by leading interactive specialists Zachary Lieberman, Theo Watson and Joel Gethin Lewis, YesYesNo aims to develop work that puts creativity and awe at the forefront of interactive media.

Acknowledgement

We would like to thank all the designers and companies who have
involved in the compilation of this book. This project would not
have been accomplished without their significant contribution to the
production of this book. We would also like to express our gratitude
to all the producers for their invaluable opinions and assistance
throughout this entire project. The successful completion also owes
a great deal to many professionals in the creative industry who have
given us precious insights and comments. And to the many others
whose names are not credited but have made specific input in this
book, we thank you for your continuous support the whole time.

Future Editions

If you wish to contribute to the next Viction:ary edition, please
email us your details to submit@victionary.com

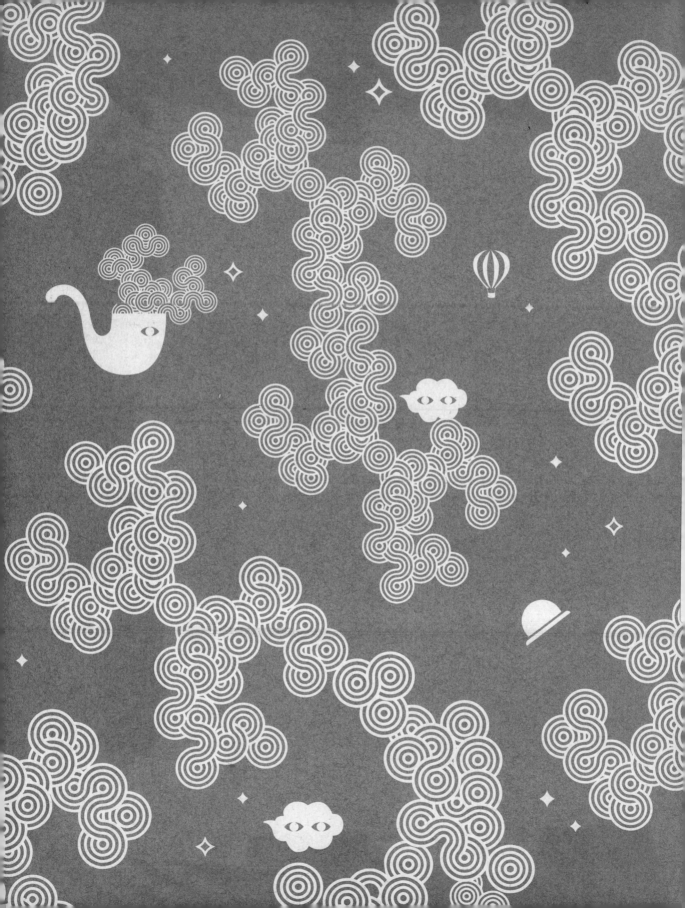